The Will to Lead

The Will to Lead

RUNNING A BUSINESS WITH A NETWORK OF LEADERS

Marvin Bower

Harvard Business School Press
Boston, Massachusetts

Library of Congress Cataloging-in-Publication Data

Bower, Marvin, 1903–
    The will to lead : running a business with a network
of leaders / Marvin Bower.
        p. cm.
    Includes index.
    ISBN 0-87584-758-7 (alk. paper)
    1. Leadership. 2. Management. I. Title.
HD57.7.B687   1997
658.4'092—dc21   96-45357
                                                       CIP

The paper used in this publication meets the requirements
of the American National Standard for Permanence of Paper
for Printed Library Materials Z39.49-1984.

Acknowledgments

From an address given by Pearl Buck. Record Group 03, Office of the President, Howard University Archives, Moorland-Spingarn Research Center.

From "Agee Payout May Exceed $2.46 Million," "Costly Lesson: GE Finds Running Kidder, Peabody & Co. Isn't All That Easy," "Gerstner Is Struggling as He Tries to Change Ingrained IBM Culture," "GM Cuts Bonuses of Top Executives, Citing Unmet Goals Despite '95 Profit," "Some Manufacturers Drop Efforts to Adopt Japanese Techniques," "Special Report on Executive Pay," and "A Tough Bank Boss Takes on Computers, with Real Trepidation." Reprinted by permission of *The Wall Street Journal,* © 1989, 1992, 1993, 1994, 1995, 1996 Dow Jones & Company, Inc. All Rights Reserved Worldwide.

From "As He Steps Down, G.M. Chairman Looks Ahead," "Big Investor Talked, Grace Listened," "Chairman To Step Down In G.M. Shift," "IBM May Quit Hilltop Headquarters," and "Procter & Gamble in 12% Job Cut as Brand Names Lose Attraction." Copyright © 1993, 94, 95 by The New York Times Co. Reprinted by Permission.

From *100 Best Companies to Work for in America* by Robert Levering and Milton Moskowitz. Copyright © 1993 by Robert Levering and Milton Moskowitz. Used by permission of Doubleday, a division of Bantam Doubleday Dell Publishing Group, Inc.

From *Sam Walton: Made in America* by Sam Walton. Copyright © 1992 by Estate of Samuel Moore Walton. Used by permission of Doubleday, a division of Bantam Doubleday Dell Publishing Group, Inc.

To Cleo
for her constant inspiration

CONTENTS

PROLOGUE
THE WILL TO LEAD:
RUNNING A BUSINESS WITH
A NETWORK OF LEADERS

This book is a "cockshy."

I learned that useful word in 1956 from John Berkin, a British managing director of Shell. Our McKinsey team had recommended a course of action, and he said, "Give me a cockshy." When I asked what that meant, John replied, "Something in writing to shoot at."

In this book we are shooting at guidelines for running a business by replacing all the "bosses" with a network of leaders and leadership teams, that is, by converting command-and-control managing to multiple leading. It has long been clear to me that some better way to manage a business is sorely needed because people don't like to be bossed under threat of firing.

I now believe that when true leaders and leadership teams are stationed strategically throughout a company, and hierarchy has been eliminated, people will be freed up to work together more effectively, efficiently, and creatively. They will exercise more initiative and get more ideas, and they will be far more likely to *want* to work together in harmony with one another and with optimism and enthusiasm, and to like their work.

I'm convinced the result will be higher-quality decision making, greater competitiveness and productivity, larger share of market, substantial improvement in profit, and greater flexibility, which will facilitate change.

I'm also convinced that in a business, leadership can be learned on the job, particularly when the chief executive, with the support of the board, decides to convert a command-and-control company to a leadership company, with everyone working together to make that change happen. I recognize that major change in a command-and-control company is usually resisted, but I believe that a major change to leading will be popular.

Clarifying Leadership

I can't prove these assertions because I have not yet found a company that motivates people *throughout* the company by leading them instead of by exercising authority and control over them. So this must be an opinion book.

For thousands of years, people have been moved by great leaders to do great things; unfortunately, people in business are not being led to do great things in their companies. Even a chief executive who is a true leader cannot make things happen throughout the company without the "scars" of hierarchy; he or she cannot get the full facts or opinions; and hierarchy blocks his or her influence from being effective throughout the company. This phenomenon has been described by John Pound, chairman of New Foundations, a multidisciplinary Harvard-based research project on corporate governance (discussed later): ". . . In hierarchical organizations, junior managers often do not feel comfortable challenging decisions because doing so might stymie their advancement. As information travels upward, bad news is filtered out. Within the corporation, then, the job of challenge falls to the CEO's peers and advisers—the directors. . . ."[1]

During the past decade, there has been so much written about "leadership"—and the term has been used so casually and loosely—that we need to clarify our terms if we are to use this cockshy to draw more fully on the great power of multiple leadership in running a business.

Let's take a typical example of confusion: When the chief executive of a business achieves outstanding results through the exercise of authority in a hierarchy of superiors and subordinates, many authors call that "leadership." I call it "managing." There is a clear and sharp distinction between "managing" people and "leading" people. And let me emphasize that it is *people* who are led, not abstract companies.

Managing a business developed essentially from military managing and works roughly this way: Chief executives have authority to run their businesses any way they and their boards wish, but most choose a hierarchy of superiors and subordinates extending to the lowest level of subordinates. Each superior in the hierarchy has authority to command and control subordinates and to fire them if they do not carry out each superior's commands or orders.

In a leadership company, leading also starts with the chief executive, who learns to become a leader so he or she can lead people to think and act through trust, example, and persuasion. Then the chief executive, with the approval of the board, plans for other leaders and leadership teams to learn leadership on the job to replace the hierarchy, in whole or in part. In simple terms, a leadership company runs the business with multiple leaders and leadership teams.

But I do want to emphasize that there are ways to run a business that fall between commanding and leading; for example, leading can be mixed with commanding to get better results than commanding would get alone. Since I believe that leadership can be learned on the job, I urge that it be tried. Using this book as a cockshy, chief executives, with the support of their boards, can custom-design ways to run their unique companies. Also, that might put their companies on the way to becoming full leadership companies.

Sources of Learning

In developing this new way of running a business, I have drawn on four principal sources.

1. *James O. McKinsey,* with whom I worked for four years until he died unexpectedly in November 1937.

From "Mac," as his friends called him, I learned basic concepts and ways of managing. Most important is the concept that making major improvements in a business can best be achieved when tackled as a whole ("holistic" is the current buzzword). Mac developed this concept from his seminal book on budgeting, published in 1922.

Mac also thought that managing should be kept as simple as possible. And the working atmosphere of a business, he believed, should be informal so as to dull the cutting edge of hierarchy.

2. *Sixty years of consulting experience*—chiefly with business firms

in the United States but a few in Europe and South America. My consulting experience with government has been limited but has been useful for contrast.

Most of this large number of corporations in a wide variety of industries were headed by chief executives who usually exercised strong authority, ranging upward to autocratic. But scattered throughout this large sample were a few CEOs and division general managers who were true leaders. I observed that the results of these units were so superior to those achieved by CEOs who exercised strong authority that the idea of developing a leadership company grew on me.

My consulting experience included writing a book published in 1966, *The Will to Manage: Corporate Success Through Programmed Management.* The purpose of that book was to improve managing through better programming. But it concludes with a short discussion of leadership:

> The best means of activating people, of course, is leadership. . . .
> When we think of "leadership" in the abstract, we are inclined to
> think of statesmen like a Lincoln or a Churchill . . . But I believe
> that *business* leadership—the only kind with which we are dealing
> here—does not require vastly superior or unusual qualities . . .[2]

So I was thinking about leading a business that far back.

3. *My own experience* in learning to lead people in McKinsey & Company, a professional firm, and adapting that experience to a business.

After Mac's death, I initiated a separation of our two eastern offices and consultants to form a new professional firm, of which I became co-head. That put me in position to learn to become a leader on the job through a process that I have adapted here to business firms.

I agree with the sidebar in a *Fortune* article (discussed later) that says in large type: "Leadership can't be taught, but can be learned."[3] Also, leadership can be self-taught, that is, a person can learn from a book—for instance, from this book—although that requires great will to lead and greater determination than most people have.

All McKinsey managing directors have become leaders on the job;

each suddenly becomes responsible for leading the firm after election by the other directors. One of our values is that we have no firm hierarchy, so all our people can speak freely and disagree with one another. Hence the managing director cannot tell people what to do. So each managing director has had to learn to lead, even though the partners work closely together in supporting one another.

4. *Intensive study* of the works of leadership scholars and of other writers on leadership. Ultimately I concluded that it was worthwhile to learn leadership behavioral principles and try to find ways to put them to work throughout a business firm.

Most scholarly writing about leadership deals largely with the field of government and politics, particularly the U.S. presidency. However, the leading scholars have gradually reached general agreement on the principles of leading. Then it became my task to determine how the basic principles of leadership could be adapted to leading everyone in a business firm. I believe that can be accomplished by combining leaders and leadership teams in the ways that I propose in this book.

There is nothing new about leadership or about teamwork. But authority is much easier to use. So it takes will, innovation, and experimentation to develop leaders and leadership teams in a business so that people can be led to work together more effectively, efficiently, and harmoniously in achieving the purpose of the business.

In a business, however, the mission or purpose of the company and the strategy and vision to achieve it are usually supplied by people at the top, although (as we shall see) leaders throughout the company can also contribute. Thus, the most difficult leadership learning is at the top. Hence a business organization is particularly well suited for people to learn leadership on the job—and for those leaders to replace bosses.

What This Book Is Not

This is not a book about leadership in general; it is confined to leading people in a business. However, many of the guidelines designed for leading people in a business can be applied to a command-and-control company to make it more effective, without having to convert it to a leadership company. This hybrid way of managing can improve performance and perhaps serve as a stepping stone to becoming a full leadership company.

This is not a "how to" book. Without companies to emulate, I cannot usefully describe the specifics for making the changes from managing with authority to running a business with leaders stationed strategically throughout the company. The specifics vary too widely among different types of companies. Thus far, I have been unable to find a leadership company counterpart to help point the way, say, for a consumer goods manufacturer, a railroad, a retailer, or any other specific type of company. Hence each company (which is really unique) must, using innovation and experimentation, develop the leadership design and specifics that will best fit its own requirements.

Getting Started

I go as far as I am able in developing leadership guidelines that, I believe, will best fit various types of businesses. That is why the book can only be a cockshy, something to shoot at.

Once a few companies—probably medium-sized or small—achieve success through multiple leading, perhaps larger companies will risk the short-term effect on stock price and follow their example. At least when I described that possibility to John Huey, managing editor of *Fortune* magazine, who has himself written about leadership, he urged me to "spit it out."

Therefore, this book is offered as a challenge to chief executives, boards of directors, top executives, middle managers, business academics, consulting firms, gurus, and B-school graduates to find the best way for particular companies to switch from managing with authority to leading people.

Although obvious, it should be said that a change of the magnitude I'm proposing cannot happen unless the chief executive has the will to lead and the support of the board of directors. However, some of the leadership proposals will be useful to chief executives, senior executives, and middle managers in improving their own personal performance in their present companies without converting the business to a leadership company.

Although I'm confident of the proposals I offer, there is one conviction I hold strongly: When a chief executive announces a program to switch from managing with authority to leading people to greater freedom, the support from these people will be enthusiastic and virtually unanimous. This conviction grows out of countless confidential discussions I have held with people about their work: People don't like to be "told"—and the closer they feel they are to self-governance, the more enthusiasm there will be for the change. Put another way, in a command company people don't normally like change, but I believe they will welcome change to a leadership company and continue to welcome it thereafter.

Once I've submitted my case for leading people in a business firm instead of commanding and controlling them, the question (for both author and reader) will be: What action will it produce? Naturally I don't want you to put this book aside to gather dust.

Yet I'm concerned that the recent flood of books on leadership has not, to my knowledge, produced even a trickle of leaders. I've tried to read most of these books, and found that many have real substantive value. Why should my book produce any greater action? Let me offer one reason for believing (or hoping) that this book will produce leadership action.

Most books on leadership are written primarily to convince the individual reader to become a leader, or at least a better manager, by developing leadership attributes. This book can do that, too, but that's not its primary purpose.

My purpose is to change the way your company is run. That takes broad *collective* action, and requires will and determination of the chief executive to lead and the approval and support of the board. However, collective action is easy to initiate—and once started in an official way, the interaction among people will, I believe, engender its own momentum, especially when the action called for is something as popular as leadership.

Marvin Bower
McKinsey & Company, Inc.
New York City

ACKNOWLEDGMENTS

EXPRESSING GRATITUDE at this point will, I believe, help readers understand this book better.

Four long-term McKinsey partners and good friends helped the most with the writing; all had higher priorities, yet found time for the book. I am most grateful.

Heading the list is Jon R. Katzenbach. He shared his great knowledge of teams, which provides the key to multiple leaders. Not only did Katz provide extensive help, but he raised my spirits. When I wondered whether going on was worthwhile, Katz was there with encouragement.

Hugh Parker took an overall view but helped particularly with the material on corporate governance (Chapter 9). He also urged me to draw more on my own experience. When we worked together in serving Shell in Venezuela in the mid-1950s, we had the good fortune to learn from the leadership example set by John Loudon, then chairman of Shell. John died early last year, before I could thank him here for his contribution to the book, but he knew how much we admired and respected him.

Steven Walleck learned long ago to express differences of opinion with me. When Steve was a young associate, we worked together in serving a client; he disagreed with the way I had negotiated the engagement with the CEO and, with my permission, renegotiated a better arrangement. So I was not surprised that, along with providing other help, Steve insisted that I clarify a number of my recommendations. I regret that Steve retired early from the firm to invest in and help run small businesses and to serve a few clients. But even with that change in priorities, he generously continued making his useful contributions to this book.

William L. Matassoni, McKinsey partner for communications, drew on his outstanding writing skills to make important editorial improvements.

Randi Zeller, partner and associate legal counsel, reviewed the manuscript. Other partners who helped are named in the text along with their contributions. Ellen Nenner, who specializes in knowledge building, helped me develop a useful example of learning leadership on the job. Specialists Anita Madison and Jim Tiberg did outstanding research and creative work.

Barbara Sinclair, my administrative assistant, and I have worked together as friends for more than 25 years. By the time I started writing the book, Barbara had long since been correcting my mistakes and suggesting improvements. Completing the book became her goal, too. Barbara has helped me in innumerable other ways over the years, always with a buoyant spirit. She passed up opportunities to move into administrative work, even though I suggested that she do so. I'm glad to have this opportunity to express my boundless gratitude.

Patricia C. Haskell, consulting editor and agent, made a most significant contribution. Pat has the great skill of making an author's style more readable without changing the author's meaning, and she knows how to make a manuscript more appealing to publishers. I'm grateful to Pat and to the author and friend who recommended her.

I had splendid help from the HBS Press, particularly from Marjorie R. Williams, executive editor, who helped shape the manuscript.

The press selected eight reviewers—CEOs and business academics—to read and report on the manuscript anonymously; and I thank them for their time, thought, and help and especially for the analytical depth of their comments. I deleted most of the passages they found weak and strengthened others. To correct the "vagueness" that several noted, I have tried to be as concrete as possible. Several suggested that I draw more broadly on my own and McKinsey experience, which I have done.

In 1992, my wife Cleo and I moved to Delray Beach, Florida, and I rented a tiny office across the street from our apartment. That provided a surprisingly quiet place to concentrate, except for occasional interruptions for firm projects or when I traveled on invitation to McKinsey offices and office retreats around North America and Europe.

I was very fortunate to be able to retain Margaret S. Neal, who served as an independent secretary, drafting material and working with Barbara in New York by telephone and through UPS service. Margaret, who has an avid interest and some experience in writing, is a member of a writers' group and a quick study. She also took over much of the mechanics of preparing this book, such as verifying footnotes, preparing permission requests, and proofing.

James O. McKinsey taught me to learn from everyone I could. And surrounded as I have been by firm and client talent, I know that there are countless others to whom I am indebted for help with the book.

Even with all this help, however, the book is still a cockshy: something for every company with the will to lead to shoot at. Since every company is unique, custom designing of the network of leaders must be done by the chief executive and top management of each particular company, although I hope that the guidelines I provide will be useful.

The Will to Lead

ONE

Why Change to Leading?

D URING THE 1980S, I participated in a major McKinsey study for a company we will call Worldwide, Inc., one of the largest in its industry, with many divisions and thousands of people working in each. The company was faltering, battered by competitors.

We began our work, as usual, with confidential interviews with top-management executives. My first assignment was to interview the general manager of the company's largest division, a man who had risen through the ranks. After some preliminary chitchat, I handed him a sheet of paper, saying: "This single page, which lists our five major professional responsibilities to clients, will give you a better understanding of McKinsey."

1. To put client interests ahead of firm interests.

2. To adhere to the highest standards of truthfulness, integrity, and trustworthiness.

3. To maintain in confidence the private and proprietary information of client organizations and any sensitive opinions of individuals within client organizations.

4. To maintain an independent position, being ready to differ with client executives and to tell them the truth as we see it, even though that may adversely affect firm income or endanger continuance of the relationship.

5. To provide only services for which the firm is competent and that provide full value for the client.

He read it carefully, looked up at the ceiling for a moment, and then said, "To understand *our* company, you should know that everyone had better damn well do what his boss tells him!" There was nothing new about his statement except its vehemence. Most people in most companies do what their bosses tell them.

The Horrors of Hierarchy

After a few days of interviewing by our people at lower levels, it was clear that people down the line were not sending up the line information of great value to the general manager I had interviewed. It was the old story of command-and-control managing, which creates a hierarchy of bosses, organized into ranks, with each superior having authority over his or her subordinates. So each subordinate does what the boss wants—or even what each subordinate *thinks* the boss wants. If you feel I exaggerate, you should have heard the general manager's people speaking in confidence to our people.

During the 60 years since I first began working with American companies to help improve their performance, there has been little basic change in the way the great majority are managed. The all-powerful CEO sits atop the hierarchy and issues orders to carry out the plans he or she has fashioned.

If you still think I exaggerate, let me tell you why that is: It's because people want to "get ahead" (i.e., move up in the hierarchy) so they can boss others. Then they can go home, tell their spouses that they have been moved up and will make more money, tell their friends, and even read their names in the papers.

Let's look more deeply at the forces at work.

How Major Change Has Perpetuated Hierarchy. Noted historian Alfred D. Chandler, Jr., in his monumental work *Strategy and Structure,*[1] defined a major change in American business through his study of changes in managing in four large enterprises: General Motors; DuPont; Standard Oil Company, New Jersey (now Exxon); and Sears, Roebuck.

From shortly after World War I on into the Great Depression, each of these great companies—working independently of one another and of any other company—created major administrative innovations to cope with the enormous expansion of the American economy that led to the rapid growth of these and other large companies.

Their reorganizations were influenced by the state of administrative art in the United States at the time. Each company thought its problems were unique and its solutions were genuine innovations. In fact, their basic conclusions were similar: a decentralized, multidivisional, profit-and-loss structure. In time, these innovations became models for similar changes in many American corporations.

I can testify to the fact that American consulting firms were called on to transport these same models across the Atlantic to large European companies. For example, this emulation had an enormous impact on the growth of McKinsey's European practice as giant corporations broke their separate businesses into profit-and-loss divisions. But each division continued to employ hierarchical, command-and-control managing. In fact, it is typical for each division general manager (or perhaps division president) to compete with the others in order to get ahead to higher rank on the basis of relative profits. Each general manager simply becomes the CEO of the divisional hierarchy.

How Incremental Change Has Perpetuated Hierarchy. Of course, there have also been thousands of incremental changes in administrative and managing methods. And growth in the use of teams (which will be dealt with later) falls somewhere between major and incremental change. Currently change of all kinds is a hot topic in managing.

But, despite these proliferating changes, the basic way most American businesses are run has changed very little over 60 years: All-powerful chief executives who report to the board still have full authority over corporate agendas; then they sit atop the hierarchies, which give them command and control over the people who execute those agendas.

Hierarchy as a Drag. The authority that each superior has over subordinates imposes these constraints on subordinates: (1) reluctance to disagree with the boss, (2) reluctance to provide information or offer opinions unless they are asked for, and (3) unwillingness to take independent initiatives. Of course, in many companies there is training directed at lessening these constraints. And good bosses will develop relationships with subordinates that virtually eliminate these constraints, although willingness of the boss to accept disagreement may not come easily.

The current use of the term "boss" is telling. Once applied only to lower-level supervisors, it is now used to refer to every superior, even the chief executive. To subordinates, the term "boss" is a constant reminder that a superior has authority over them. Superiors have responsibilities to evaluate subordinates for compensation and advancement. So because subordinates want to get ahead and move up in the hierarchy, they take great care to do what their bosses say—or even seem to indicate. Moreover, the boss can define the subordinate's standing in the company and can, of course, fire subordinates.

Further, getting ahead motivates superiors and subordinates to think about how their decisions and actions will affect them personally. Indeed, this is perhaps the most important negative feature of the command system, but also its basic strength.

By holding bosses individually responsible for getting the job done, by making them accountable for each subordinate's job performance, by giving them the authority to evaluate the subordinate's job performance and determine his or her future compensation and advancement, the command system does get results.

Nevertheless, hierarchy is so poorly regarded that many able people shy away from joining large companies. Recently I participated in four classes of second-year students at Harvard Business School, about half the graduating class. Three-quarters of them had worked in large corporations for an average of four years before coming to HBS. They so disliked hierarchy that most were seeking employment in small companies (suggesting a frightening diversion of talent that large companies can ill afford).

At a time when a company needs every person to be totally involved in helping to improve company performance, hierarchy compels decision makers, at every level, to consider their personal interests as well as the company's interests. This has been proven to me over the years. Of my confidential interviews with client executives at all levels (except for those at the highest level), a significant percentage of them have ended this way: "Before we finish, do you have any suggestions on how I might get ahead faster?" with some adding: "I'm thinking of leaving the company because I'm not moving ahead fast enough."

The Tide Is Turning

Many American chief executives are now recognizing the severe shortcomings of command-and-control managing. However, the cry for basic change was stronger a few years ago. General Electric began telling shareholders about substantial changes in managing methods in the late 1980s. In his 1991 chairman's letter, John F. Welch, Jr., chairman, and Edward E. Hood, Jr., vice chairman, condemned command-and-control managing by saying, "Layers insulate. They slow things down. They garble. Leaders in highly layered organizations are . . . blissfully ignorant of the realities of their environment."[2]

In 1990, in the *Harvard Business Review*, Elmer Johnson, senior partner in the law firm of Kirkland & Ellis in Chicago and a former executive vice president and board member of General Motors, said: "One of history's most remarkable organizational achievements—the large public corporation, governed by an independent board of directors—has served society for most of this century as an unrivaled creator of wealth and employment. Now it is an endangered species, and we must take strong measures to preserve and renew it."[3]

The shock that IBM and other icons could be among the endangered species does, indeed, call for strong measures. Responding to the cries of security analysts and heavy investors to change the chief executives of faltering companies, most boards ultimately do make a change. (Within the past few years, chief executives of IBM, General Motors, Westinghouse, American Express, and Eastman Kodak, among others, have been forced out.)

In 1992, among the Fortune 100 largest industrial companies, the chairmen's letters to shareholders in their annual reports clearly indicated that nothing less than a minor revolution was afoot in the way that large American companies were being managed. Wayne

Calloway, then CEO of PepsiCo, said it outright: "I believe there's a consumer revolution taking place across the globe and that's why we must redefine how we do business."[4]

That year, other chief executives were not satisfied with the way their businesses were being run, and in their letters to stockholders said so strongly. In their annual report letter, Lawrence Bossidy, chairman, and Alan Belzer, president, of Allied-Signal, Inc., wrote: ". . . success in the 1990s will involve fundamental changes in how we operate our businesses and in the way each of us understands his or her role in the Company. . . . [Management is in] the process of 'reinventing' Allied-Signal."[5]

In all, 26 of the 100 shareholder letters in 1992 expressed the same message as Allied-Signal. Paul H. O'Neill, chairman and CEO of Alcoa, said, "This reorganization sheds the layered approvals and delays of a command-and-control structure. . . ."[6]

Dissatisfied with the state of the command-and-control system, many other companies, though not reinventing or transforming the way they run their businesses, have nevertheless been making changes to improve the system.

The managements of most large and medium-sized American companies are making changes in their managing systems because they recognize that they are now handicapped by the way they are managing and fear that they will find themselves even further handicapped in the near future. They are striving for greater effectiveness and flexibility to cope with, and even capitalize on, the fast-moving, ever-changing competitive conditions they see now or know lie just ahead.

But in all the cries for change, I have not heard any call for leadership to replace authority. Of course, there have been many books on leadership, but most seem to focus on helping individuals become leaders, not on ways to run the business through a network of leaders.

In these pages I have endeavored to think through a process for first learning to lead on the job, and then developing a design for a network of individual leaders and leadership teams to work together in running the company.

I believe that leaders and leadership teams working together in a proper design will run the business more effectively than by hierarchical, command-and-control managing. But I can't prove that. And there are no models. Thus, each management must develop a custom design for running its particular company through a network of leaders, that is, make leadership effective *throughout* the company.

Over time, I believe the command system must be replaced. "Fixing it" is not good enough. However, replacement won't be easy. It probably won't happen until smaller companies lead the way—until they demonstrate that their networks of leaders can compete successfully with command-and-control companies.

Chief executives who are now "bosses" (and that's most of them) must develop the will to lead by making a personal commitment to leading: by themselves developing leadership qualities and attributes specific to the business, and by developing (and leading) networks of leaders and leadership teams stationed strategically throughout their companies. Again, that's what this book is shooting at.

Leading a Business

Throughout history, leaders have moved the world by leading people. Leaders founded the United States and fashioned documents to guide other leaders that have made the nation outstandingly successful for more than two hundred years.

Why, then, have leaders not taken on the overall running of business corporations? Of course, many chief executives of business corporations have been true leaders. But they have not set out to develop other leaders to manage the company as a whole. Authority is too easy to use; and our laws support its use. Perhaps because becoming a leader in the public arena is recognized as difficult, so is it considered difficult in a business. Why, then, learn to lead when authority gets the job done?

Leadership scholars define a leader (usually a political leader) as a person who sets attractive goals and has the abilities to attract followers, or *constituents,* who have the same goals. Political leaders (e.g., a president or governor) must have the qualities and attributes required to achieve their common goals. But above all, the leader must be trusted and respected. Indeed, the heart of leadership is mutual trust between leaders and constituents. As they work together, trust opens up two-way communication, making it possible for them to achieve their common goals.

Actually, I believe that leading in a business is much easier to understand, learn, and implement than it is in the political arena. In a business, constituents don't need to be attracted; they are already company employees. However, the leader-constituent relationship develops only when the potential leader earns the trust of constituents, thereby engendering mutual trust. Only then do leaders and constituents have open, two-way communications as they decide together and work together to achieve the (company) goals they have in common.

When a company decides to run its business by leading its people rather than commanding them, constituents will feel free to exercise initiatives, express opinions to their leaders, innovate, and even disagree with their leaders. The impediments of hierarchy will have been removed. Also, in establishing company purpose and developing company strategy and vision, the chief executive will then have the help of leaders and constituents throughout the company. Leadership will then have been "institutionalized."

Indeed, in a leadership company, leaders of teams (positioned strategically throughout the company) do not provide their constituents with answers. Instead, leaders and constituents work out decisions and take actions together. And that's why leadership improves performance more dramatically than hierarchical, command-and-control managing.

TWO

A Personal Learning Journey

I LEARNED LEADERSHIP on the job in an amateurish way: by trial and error, and without knowing the principles of leadership. Because many of my suggestions in these pages depend on my own judgments and opinions, you might find them more credible if I tell you, briefly, what I did before I joined McKinsey, and something about my hands-on experience in learning to lead once I was there.

Developing My Goal

I learned later that every leader must have a goal. As you will see, mine developed in an unexpected and roundabout way. After graduating from Brown University in 1925, I had no idea what to do for a career. My father, who knew many lawyers, told me that a legal education provides a good basis for many other careers. I went to Harvard Law School. My father also suggested to a lawyer friend that he give me summer jobs with his firm while I was in law school, and this respected firm (in Cleveland, Ohio, where I grew up) took me on.

During my summers, many partners in that firm often spoke of another Cleveland firm now known as Jones, Day, Reavis & Pogue, then and now the leading corporate firm in the area. Their admiration was so genuine that I decided I would try to join Jones Day. But, alas, Jones Day turned me down because I did not make the *Law Review*. So I decided to go to Harvard Business School, make the *Business Review* there (which was then student edited), and try again at Jones Day.

Before my graduation in 1928, however, I was summoned to the office of Roscoe Pound, the school's eminent dean. As I entered, he was sitting at the end of a long table. Always brusque, he started right out.

"Bower," he said, "I have a job for you with the general counsel's office of International Paper."

"Thank you, Dean," I said, "but I don't want a job. I'm going to Harvard Business School in the fall."

He stared at me. "My God, Bower, you are about to graduate from the greatest educational institution in the world, and now you're going to *that* place?" He pointed across the Charles River, picked up a book, and threw it the length of his table. That's what academia thought of business as a career in the late twenties.

I went to the Business School and made the *Review* at the end of the first year. Then I started wondering whether the second year was worth the time and money. I decided to take an opinion survey of a dozen people, including a J. P. Morgan partner; from that firm I selected Arthur Marvin Anderson on the basis of his middle name.

The guard at 23 Wall Street asked what I wanted, and Mr. Anderson saw me immediately. I put my question, and without hesitating, Mr. Anderson said, "If you don't finish the second year, you will spend the rest of your life explaining that you did not flunk out."

I told him that his judgment was overwhelming and that I would finish. When I thanked him and rose to go, he asked what I was going to do for the summer. I said I hoped to get a job. Would I, he asked, like to work for Morgan's law firm, Davis, Polk & Wardwell, located in the adjacent building? He arranged for me to go right up, and after two hours of interviews with several partners I had a summer job.

My wife, Helen, and I spent the roaring summer of 1929 in New York City. My work was all on mergers, including Standard Brands, and I had several legal greats as mentors.

I finished the second year at HBS. I had an offer of a job with Davis Polk, but Jones Day also came through, and I reported there for work in June 1930.

The Jones Day Years

After having spent extra time and effort to get the job, naturally I wondered what made Jones Day so great. Over the next two years, I listened, observed, and talked with other young associates. I was also lucky enough to work for the senior partner and three other "rainmakers" (the ones who bring in clients).

My findings were uniform. Every one of the partners met the highest professional standards, which basically meant they put the client's interests ahead of the firm's. All were careful to maintain confidences. All were independent: They never took on an assignment unless it was really necessary and could not be handled just as well by a client's house counsel. They were always ready to disagree with client people if that was in the client's interest and were always creative in handling legal matters so effectively that fees were kept low. Indeed, these partners frequently made creative suggestions about the client's business that had nothing to do with their legal matters.

And among us associates, all four partners I worked for were notable for on-the-job coaching. I can't recall an occasion when I took a piece of work to one of these partners that he didn't spend five to ten minutes telling me how it could be improved—and also how my work might square better with the firm's policies for serving clients.

But one incident made the biggest impression of all. The head of an investment banking firm came to the senior partner with a plan for merging two companies. The senior partner asked for a few days to research the antitrust aspects. When the prospective client returned, the senior partner told him the antitrust risks were too great, and declined the assignment, even though the banker said his firm was willing to take fee risks up to $1 million (a lot of money during the Great Depression). The banker went to another law firm, which took the assignment. After running up several hundred thousand dollars of legal fees, the banking firm went bankrupt and the law firm collected nothing.

That rare example of independence was so compelling that, together with my other experience with these four partners, it became clear why the partners of the competing firm admired Jones Day. It was no wonder that Jones Day clients recommended the firm to other companies. There was no secret to its success: high-value work for clients while adhering to high professional standards and gaining and maintaining the confidences of clients.

My legal practice at Jones Day also provided an interesting reward for the two extra years at Harvard Business School.

The Great Depression was deepening, and many industrial companies in the Cleveland area were beginning to default on their bonds but not go into bankruptcy. Instead, bondholders organized committees comprising bankers and investment bankers. These committees took control of the companies, wiping out the common stock and superseding the boards of directors. Jones Day became counsel to many committees, and because I had gone to Harvard Business School, I was made secretary of some ten committees.

I was only a young law clerk, but as secretary to these committees I was perceived to have substantial authority. And to an extent I had: I had full access to the chief executives and anybody else who could contribute to my work. Because the role of each committee was to reorganize the company, I studied each company's potential earning power and prepared drafts of reorganization plans for the committees. I gained broad knowledge of how these companies were managed and deep insights into people's behavior in a business setting.

I realized that my studies of these businesses and their managing problems were amateurish and superficial. But an insight emerged from the experience: Just as there was a need for independent advice to business firms on legal problems, I perceived there was also a real need and opportunity for a consulting firm giving independent advice on managing problems. In other words, independent consultants on managing could help improve business performance and would be more likely to be retained if they met the professional standards of Jones Day and thus gained the trust of clients. That became my goal.

In fact, I began discussing with my wife the great opportunities and also great risk of switching from the law to consulting on managing.

The McKinsey Early Years

Early in 1933, I met James O. McKinsey in Chicago while working for a bondholders' committee of a company headquartered there. "Mac," as he was known, headed James O. McKinsey and Company, an "accounting and engineering" firm that gave managing advice to business firms. Mentor of young people that he was, Mac asked me about my career. The upshot of our meeting was that, after many discussions with McKinsey partners and my wife, I decided to take a real risk and change careers by joining McKinsey's tiny New York office in 1933, to become a professional consultant on managing. This, I believed, would put me in position to pursue my goal. I had told Mac about the kind of professional consulting I wanted to practice, and he could see the logic of it.

Thus, I brought to McKinsey the idea that had emerged from study of the law and work with bondholders' committees at Jones Day. (What I then called an "idea" would today be called a "vision.") It embodied the five professional responsibilities for serving consulting clients that I listed in Chapter 1 and gave to a client executive. These were distilled from the code of responsibilities for serving legal clients. I had observed that holding to these responsibilities had worked well in the law to attract and gain the trust of clients, and I believed they would work even better in the new—and unrecognized—field of consulting on managing.

I could not actively pursue my goal immediately, however; I was too busy serving McKinsey clients, working mostly with Mac and learning much from him. Also, in late 1934, I was made manager of the tiny New York office, which had three other consultants. Shortly thereafter came the largest and most important consulting engagement the firm had ever had—an overall study of Marshall Field & Company, the big Chicago retailer, which then had several other businesses. I was Mac's lieutenant in guiding our team. Our report was delivered in May 1935.

The board of directors accepted our recommendations, which involved enormous change. Then the board asked Mac to take over as chief executive, with the understanding that he would return to McKinsey after our recommendations had been carried out.

Mac Leaves, Mergers Follow

The news of Mac's new job at Marshall Field brought a dozen letters offering to merge with our "one-man" firm. The largest was Scovell, Wellington, an accounting and consulting firm, headquartered in New York, with 13 offices, headed by C. Oliver Wellington, a handsome man of great integrity but, as we would learn later, a real autocrat. The consulting group was headed by Horace Guy Crockett (Guy), also a man of great integrity and a fine and able person in his mid-fifties.

Mac was eager to get started at Field's. So, over a weekend, he and Oliver decided to set up two interlocking partnerships: Scovell, Wellington (SW) for accounting and McKinsey, Wellington (MW) for consulting. Oliver was managing partner of both firms. There were no other formal relations between the two firms, but there were interlocking partners: Oliver, Mac, Guy, and Dick Fletcher, head of consulting in Boston. In addition to the interlocking partners, the MW firm had five other partners: A. T. Kearney, head of the Chicago office; three other Chicago partners representing the large Chicago staff; and me, representing the small New York staff. Several of us objected, but the shotgun marriage went right ahead.

Guy became head of the MW consulting group. Even though he was old enough to be my father, Guy and I got along fine on a sort of co-head basis. We kept our MW office separate from the other firm, and Oliver kept his New York office where it had always been. Most of the merging took place in the New York office because most of the Scovell consultants were in the East.

It did not take long, however, for Oliver to command and (try to) control the large Chicago group of MW partners and associates. Tom Kearney led the resentment. I stood up to Oliver, and Guy supported me because he liked the casual, fun culture that Mac had established. Guy and I had made that the culture of the whole consulting group, which was easy because everyone liked it. And our people still do.

Looking back I can now see that we had a sort of in-house example of the difference between a command-and-control and a leadership culture. Geography helped a lot, and despite the culture gap, MW prospered in attracting and serving clients. But before the inevitable break, there was tragedy: Mac died unexpectedly from pneumonia in November 1937.

Tom Kearney proposed we unmerge, and that all partners return to their original firms and offices. I said that I hoped we might hold the consulting firm together, and Guy agreed. Oliver had no proposal.

It was logical that I negotiate with Tom Kearney because I knew him well and liked him greatly. But we found we had different goals. I insisted that we be a professional firm; Tom wanted an ethical firm, of course, but was indifferent to the other "professional" standards listed in Chapter 1. I wanted to expand to a national firm with offices in all sections of the country. Tom thought the Chicago area provided a sufficiently large base of potential clients. I wanted to recruit high-talent young people and train them; Tom wanted to hire senior people, even former vice presidents. We got nowhere.

So Guy went to Chicago to negotiate with Tom. He got nowhere. We had reached an impasse.

After thinking carefully and talking with my wife, we decided that I would suggest to Guy that we break away from the Chicago group and go it alone with our Eastern group. To my amazement, Guy said yes immediately, even though he would have to put up most of our small capital and we knew we would have to operate in the red for a while.

Now that I have studied leadership principles, I believe I know why Guy agreed so readily, although we never discussed it. First, he trusted me because we both believed in professional responsibilities and had followed them together. Second, we had come to agree that as a professional firm we would have competitive advantage over other consulting firms. Third, he would become head of the new firm and would not have to return to taking orders from Oliver and work in his kind of culture.

The separation arrangements were easy to negotiate because they were among partners. Even Oliver was broad-gauged. Our use of the McKinsey name came later when Tom Kearney agreed to the name A. T. Kearney & Company.[1] And leaving aside many important but irrelevant details, our new firm was ready, in the fall of 1939, to become a separate, distinctive professional firm to help companies improve their managing performance.

We organized as a legal partnership, which meant that any partner could bind the firm, and that all partners were legally liable. That put all of our personal assets at risk, which meant that we all had to trust one another implicitly. That level of trust brought us close together personally, and I have never forgotten the meaning of "partnership."

We borrowed money, brought in one new partner, advanced people to partnership from within, and had good luck in attracting new clients whose fees brought us out of the red. Guy and I divided the responsibilities: He managed day-to-day operations and I worked on long-range opportunities. And we both served clients. So we were sort of co-heads, although he was the real head.

Facing the Professional Challenge

Now I had the opportunity to achieve the goal I had set before I left the law. There were no objections from the partners about becoming a professional firm, but to become a professional firm instead of a commercial firm requires real belief in professional standards and determination to follow them. "Commercial" means putting firm income ahead of client interests, and this is a fine line to draw when the firm is on the edge of losing money or when people have vaulted financial ambitions.

How would I convince the partners and associates that the professional approach was the way to go? I had no real authority. I had never run anything except the tiny New York office for about a year, and then I was away a lot on consulting engagements. So I just took the initiative and started advocating the professional approach in meetings and in memorandums—in fact, I pounded pretty hard.

Then two partners took me aside separately, and told me I could not achieve my goals by ordering it done. I thanked them. They believed in the professional approach themselves and said that they would advocate it with others—but that I should take off the pressure. I did. Instead, I observed what people did and commended anyone who followed the professional approach.

As we went along, I noted that people increasingly asked me questions about how the professional approach should be applied. For example, just what did "independence" mean? In explaining that it could involve disagreeing with client people, I pointed out that disagreement is important to top management because people in the client company are reluctant to disagree with their bosses. Later when I learned about leadership, I found that leaders are always receptive to questions.

Prospective clients began to respond positively. We found that we were more likely to be retained when we took an independent position, that is, when we exercised the courage to disagree with prospective client people when we felt that was in their company's interests. So we gained their confidence and increased our own. Clients adopted more of our recommendations because they believed us; they knew we were not trying to "sell" them (get more work from them) but to persuade them to do what we really believed was in their best interests.

Whenever I could, I tried to use positive examples and watch carefully how people responded. I described favorable developments within the firm and with clients to our partners and associates and observed their reactions. I tried never to say anything that would be considered an order. And I found that it was increasingly easy to make suggestions, that is, to persuade people. So I stepped up persuasion.

I knew nothing then about the principles of leading. Of course from reading history and biography, I knew that leaders have great power to make things happen. But nothing I learned at Harvard Business School had told me that leadership as such could make things happen in a business. Then, as now, managing was based on authority. Privately, I came to call the process I was using "persuasion through pointing up success." Years later, after I had studied the leadership scholars, it became clear that what I had been doing was learning to lead—and I found it much easier to learn than people often think.

True, I benefited from the power of example: Most of the partners had either had firsthand experience with Oliver Wellington and Mac

McKinsey or had heard about them—and they much preferred Mac's way of leading over Oliver's way of ordering. And as we established commitment to our five professional responsibilities to clients, we also developed guiding principles, strategy, and policies to lead our people into supporting and discharging these responsibilities.

We found that the professional approach also helped us attract the talented people we need to serve clients, and whom we could develop and motivate. All this gave us a strong focus for serving clients in an outstanding fashion. In my view, that same focus can, through leadership, be established in a commercial business because leading people to serve customers in an outstanding way is, I believe, the purpose of every business.

The Harvey Golub Story

This brings me to Harvey Golub, now chief executive of American Express.

Harvey joined McKinsey in our New York office in 1966. He was very successful and became a director early. One of the clients he served was American Express, and one of the studies he directed for that client was an evaluation of its prospective acquisition of Investors Diversified Services (IDS), a mutual fund sold door to door. The acquisition was made; the client decided that IDS required a new chief executive and offered the job to Harvey; we were sorry that he took it. Because the job also took him to Minneapolis, I saw little of him.

As years went along, I was pleased to hear of the great success Harvey was having in running IDS. Then, one day, he unexpectedly called to arrange dinner with me in New York. When we met, he said he wanted to tell me why he had been successful at IDS, and then, in some detail, he described how that success was based on training the IDS organization to run its business by the values he had learned at McKinsey. These were gratifying words, but the values that Harvey had learned at McKinsey were simply professional values that any good lawyer would follow.

However, the people in Harvey's company were trained to follow these simple values, and to that Harvey attributes IDS's outstanding success. In my view, the principles of leadership in a business are also simple for people to learn, and when leadership is spread around a company, it can have a powerful effect on what people can accomplish by working closely together.

Because this chapter has dealt with McKinsey's becoming a professional firm, however, does not mean I advocate that for a command company. Nevertheless, because leadership is based on trust, there will be, and should be, some resemblance between a professional firm and a leadership company. And the more the type of business calls for trust, the greater that resemblance should be.

For example, financial businesses are shot through with the need for trust and hence should be run more like professional firms. Even an insurance company that acquires a securities business should run the joint business in that manner to avoid fraud. That is how Harvey Golub achieved success with IDS.

The purpose of the next five chapters is twofold: first, to show how the process of learning to lead works, and second, to show how leading can so permeate a business that it no longer needs to depend solely on leadership from one person at the top; leadership will then bubble up from all parts of the business. In short, Chapters 3 through 7 show how leadership can be institutionalized to operate throughout a company.

THREE

Developing Leaders in a Business

IN THIS CHAPTER, I define a set of leadership qualities and attributes that I believe will serve as cockshies for leaders in running a business. Although designed for a leadership company, I believe these leadership qualities and attributes will be useful for strengthening any company no matter how it is being run now, even by command and control.

But first some definition. The word "qualities" means elements of character or personal makeup that are typically difficult (but not always impossible) to learn, for example, to change a person's behavior. Indeed, people usually bring their qualities with them on joining the company, whereas "attributes" are more like skills and hence easier to learn. But neither term can be precise. I'm pleased, however, that attributes (the easier ones) far outnumber the qualities.

Most potential leaders in a business will have acquired many of the basic qualities and attributes before joining the company, even early in life: at home, in school, in sports, or while working in their early jobs. Most will have used many of them as managers. And I believe that potential leaders in a business can learn most attributes on the job fairly easily, provided they have the will and determination to do so, and the example of overall leadership provided by the chief executive and other leaders. So let's first take up the role of CEO.

The Chief Executive Learning to Lead

The chief executive must set the example for all other company leaders to follow.

I believe that most chief executives will be quick studies in learning leadership. After working with as many CEOs as I have, I believe that most (clearly not all) will have no great difficulty in switching from being bosses to becoming leaders. Nearly all will have a number of well-defined leadership qualities and attributes simply because the boards that chose them will have used many leadership qualities as selection criteria, even though the board's objective may have been to select a command-and-control type—a "boss."

The CEO who wants to learn to lead simply begins to act like a leader by actually demonstrating leadership qualities and attributes on the job, and by observing how subordinates react. For example, I'm confident that if the CEO begins listening (as a leader does and most bosses don't), the CEO will be surprised and exhilarated by the positive reactions of subordinates.

Again, the CEO, or any other learning leader, should *act* like a leader, and then observe what happens. For instance, if the CEO or other learning leader comes to be trusted, constituents will act differently: They will feel free (even delighted) to have open discussions with the new leader (formerly boss). I can well remember the positive signals I received when I was learning to lead in McKinsey.

Looking back, I can think of many chief executives who had the *qualities* for leading and, if they had had the will, could easily have acquired the few attributes that would have made them genuine leaders. But I can also think of others who, though not dishonest, did not meet ethical standards that would gain the trust of their subordinates, and were devious and/or self-serving. The CEOs in the latter group could manage successfully with authority, but lacked the trust to lead the company.

So I suggest that chief executives who have the qualities for leading experiment with learning the *attributes* that will make them leaders. (I'm not suggesting here that they convert their companies to leadership companies unless that develops naturally.) This experiment would have two advantages. First, the chief executive would become a better boss, and there is real advantage for a CEO to be a leader in a command company. Second, the chief executive would gain firsthand experience in assessing the difficulties of the learning process for other potential leaders.

Let me describe another McKinsey leadership learning experience. Even though it took place in a professional firm, I believe that people in many businesses can learn to lead from it nonetheless.

As D. Ronald Daniel, then firm managing director, was nearing the end of his term, he and others concluded that the firm needed a greater organized effort to build knowledge covering the entire field of managing, thus expanding and strengthening our practice development. Frederick W. Gluck, a director, was especially vocal in advocating that the firm move aggressively to build and strengthen our knowledge and expertise in areas of greatest concern to our clients, to index it so our worldwide firm could draw on it, and develop the best ways for communicating the knowledge. Shortly thereafter, Fred became the driving force in this effort.

This monumental effort required that a large number of consultants spend about 15 percent of their time on knowledge building—and some even more—while forgoing an equivalent amount of time in serving clients. This they were reluctant to do, because it meant substituting "staff" work for "line" work. Since we have no hierarchy in the firm, Fred could not order consultants to expend the knowledge-building time. So he had to turn to leadership to achieve the goal.

First, he set an example by eliminating all of his own client time. Then he defined the importance to the firm of the new knowledge-building goal: improved quality of client work, more new ideas, and faster training of new consultants. Next he communicated his vision throughout the firm.

Knowledge building was divided into fields of practice, and an interested and qualified person was put in charge of each. Fred gave each practice leader some initial guidance, but he was not a boss. The success or failure of knowledge building for each practice area was each leader's individual responsibility. And Fred also prepared for a second generation of practice leaders.

He took every opportunity to make the new knowledge-building effort widely known throughout the firm through presentations at meetings, conferences, and office retreats. As the new knowledge-building effort proved its value to clients, it gained the support of everyone and the enthusiasm of the knowledge builders.

Fred was always accessible and took time to speak with people who had problems and concerns. He loved what he was doing, and his enthusiasm for practice development was always evident. He made everyone who worked with him a believer.

Practice leaders were encouraged to take risks to improve quality. And Fred praised them when they made rapid progress or achieved unusual results. Thus the practice leaders set examples throughout the firm.

Over a number of years, practice development leadership and involvement became institutionalized within the firm—an integral part of McKinsey's culture and value system. Those who participated derived great personal benefit and satisfaction. Meantime, Fred was elected managing director by secret ballot.

I believe that people in many businesses who are determined to become leaders can benefit from Fred's leadership learning experience.

The Qualities and Attributes of Leading

I have selected the following qualities and attributes of leading for a business from the writings of leadership scholars, with adaptations when needed.

As I explained earlier, the way to determine whether you, the chief executive, and other learning leaders are being recognized or accepted as leaders by constituents is by observing how they react to changes in your behavior. For example, if you begin listening, constituents will react positively; then you will know you are recognized for your leadership.

To become a chief executive, you must develop all (or nearly all) these qualities and attributes; less important leaders need not learn them all or as thoroughly.

Trustworthiness. Leadership scholars are virtually unanimous in putting trustworthiness at the top of the list of qualities required by any leader. The chief executive should have little difficulty in receiving positive signals from constituents or direct reports, because he or she will clearly have been selected by the board for having qualities that make him or her trustworthy. All others who seek to become leaders will have to prove their trustworthiness through the reactions of *their* constituents to their truthfulness.

When I became a constituent of Mac McKinsey in 1933, I knew I was taking a risk. I was leaving an outstanding firm in a respected profession to join a small, new firm in an unrecognized field—and during the Great Depression. I followed Mac as a leader because I trusted him. I liked him and sensed that he liked me. From our several meetings before I joined, I felt he could be trusted not to let me get into a situation that had no chance of working out well for me.

Mac had been completely forthright in describing the firm and its outlook, and I sensed that he was speaking truthfully. He used no pressure on me to join the firm, and I tested his sincerity by refusing to take a lower salary than I was making, even though it was higher than salaries in the firm I would be joining. Clearly his goals and mine were similar, and I felt he would help me achieve mine.

After I joined, I found Mac to be everything I had expected and hoped for. During the few years we worked closely together, he was always forthright; he never stretched the truth; he was never devious. In hindsight, he was a genuine leader, and the quality of his leadership was an important legacy to McKinsey & Company.

Ron Daniel, an outstanding leader who was McKinsey's managing director from 1976 to 1988, had this to say at a conference of McKinsey partners:

> My message—in talking about how leaders and followers interact—is a simple one:
>
> - I believe that a follower in looking to a leader must have (1) professional respect for him and (2) personal trust in him—if the leader is to be effective in his role.
>
> - Respect and trust, however, are only the price of admission. Beyond that a leader must demonstrate behavior that suggests (1) a willingness to make a real investment in the professional development of junior people and (2) a genuine concern for the junior person as a human being.
>
> - These interactions between leaders and followers are fueled and facilitated by active and regular communications.[1]

Trustworthiness is integrity in action. Pearl S. Buck, winner of the 1938 Nobel Prize for Literature, was right on the mark when, in a lecture for the Ghandi Foundation, she said: "Integrity is honesty carried through the fibers of the being and the whole mind, into thought as well as into action so that the person is complete in honesty. That kind of integrity I put above all else as an essential of leadership."[2]

In his powerful book *The Moral Sense,*[3] James Q. Wilson also says that trust is based on truthfulness and honesty. This squares with my experience in working with chief executives I knew to be leaders. Dr. Wilson's research shows that most children learn through very early experience that untruthfulness and dishonesty do not pay off, and that if the lesson doesn't carry over into adulthood, most people ultimately learn it then. That's why Dr. Wilson says that a high proportion of our population is truthful.

Finally, to be trustworthy, anyone seeking to be a leader should always tell the truth if for no other reason than it is simpler. When we were working together as officers in a nonprofit organization during a critical situation, my friend Richard Heckert, now retired chairman of DuPont and a real leader, put it this way: "If you always tell the truth, you won't have to remember what you said."

I have observed that executives I trusted most were truthful about unimportant as well as important things. Those who were trustworthy went into detail to be accurate about small things, even correcting statements about things that did not matter. In other words, they used "high-precision" truthfulness because they found that, as Dr. Wilson says, high-quality truthfulness establishes trust.

High-precision truthfulness is a good way to gain trust, the ticket of admission to leadership.

Let me give another example: An experience of Ralph Hart, a good friend who died in 1995, who was formerly chairman of Heublein and earlier president of Colgate-Palmolive Co. In 1994 Ralph was one of the recipients of the Horatio Alger Award.

In his biography for the award, he told of an incident early in his career. He had been hired to sell adding machines to small stores. He was given no training, but was provided with sample machines and immediately sent into the field. When he began his route, he was too nervous to enter the first store. As it was late in the day, he decided to wait until morning and begin fresh. But the next day, he was still too nervous to attempt a sale. Finally, near closing time, he approached a store owner, who wasn't interested. In Ralph's words:

> I asked, "Would you at least look at them?" So the store owner started asking me questions, and I kept on saying, "I don't know, but I'll find out." Finally the owner agreed to purchase an adding machine. I was mystified, and asked him why he finally relented. He replied, "Anyone who has a salesman as honest as you are must have a good product." That was one of the greatest things that ever happened to me. It's something I never forgot—be honest and tell the truth.[4]

Fairness. Over the years, as a consultant, the most frequent complaint about bosses made to me (in confidence) has been some form of unfairness. To get something done, the boss had used authority carelessly: In the eyes of subordinates what the boss wanted done was unnecessary, too difficult, or impossible in the time given.

In America, to be called an "unfair" boss is damning, and even implies a flawed character. Conversely, a boss who is "tough but fair" is a character to be admired. In our dictionaries, fairness in behavior is variously defined as equitable, unprejudiced, impartial, dispassionate, objective. Dr. Wilson says that "fairness has one or more of three meanings: equity, reciprocity, and impartiality."[5]

However it is defined, Americans—possibly because of their intense involvement in sports—are quick to recognize what's fair and what's unfair. They will forgive much, but seldom unfairness. Unfairness in a chief executive is particularly serious, because he or she sets the example for everyone else in the company.

Fairness and trust, of course, go hand in hand. Both are essential not only in the chief executive but in all leaders throughout the company. Moreover, if fairness and trust become an integral part of a company's culture, then these qualities will flourish to the company's great benefit.

Let me cite the origin of a policy of fairness at McKinsey & Company that continues to have an extraordinary impact on the firm 50 years after we initiated it. In 1944, we opened our third office by transferring a small cadre of experienced people from the New York office to San Francisco: They knew our values, our strategy, and our ways of serving clients. We had no way of knowing how long it would take for the new office to have earnings that could be distributed as bonuses. But we decided, rather easily, that the only fair thing to do was to pool the earnings of all three offices and divide the total bonus money equitably (on the basis of meritocracy) among the consultants in all offices.

We concluded that this was also the fair thing to do from the standpoint of the New York office. New York had sacrificed the earning power of outstanding consultants who were now in San Francisco, and it was only fair that their earning power should not be completely lost. This, too, was accomplished by pooling the earnings of all offices and compensating individuals on the basis of performance, thereby making it fairer to those individuals who were asked to move to San Francisco, and were therefore more willing to transfer. The New York partners were also more willing to give them up.

Out of these decisions, all rooted in fairness, we developed our one-firm concept, which applies today to all our offices. We treat each office as a part of the whole firm. Because we are strongly committed to meritocracy, we make senior advancements on a firmwide basis. Our performance for clients has been improved by our ability to transfer experienced people to new offices and develop highly effective teams with members of various competencies drawn from an array of offices.

When we transfer a cadre of experienced people to a new office, we immediately employ consultants and support staff from nationals of the new (to us) country—and try to demonstrate that they will be treated fairly.

When we opened our London office, for example, we at first had difficulty employing high-talent nationals as consultants. Other American consulting firms had opened London offices and then closed them. Candidates thought we might, too. But more important, they felt that when it came to advancement they would be treated unfairly, that is, in choosing between an American and a Briton, we would not be impartial.

Over time we convinced high-talent people to join, but it was not until we actually advanced British nationals over Americans that skepticism about our fairness faded. Once we proved our fairness in the United Kingdom, however, we had less difficulty in attracting foreign nationals in our offices on the Continent. And once we had non-Americans as managers of non-American offices (which is and always was our objective), the fairness of McKinsey was genuinely accepted.

In 1994, by secret ballot of all senior partners (our long-term policy), we elected Rajat Gupta, an Indian-born, naturalized American, as managing director of the firm. He is a leader and we all gladly became his constituents.

Among our current 69 offices, we have citizens of 77 countries. It is astonishing that despite their many different national cultures, we experience no serious problems in interpreting fairness.

Unassuming Behavior. Arrogance, haughtiness, and egotism are poisonous to leadership. But leaders can never be hypocritically humble. They are simply unassuming in their behavior. Unpretentiousness can be learned, and it is well suited to the examples the chief executive should set.

My late friend, Robert K. Greenleaf, former director of managing research for AT&T, developed a useful reminder for being an unassuming leader: "servant leadership." In a pamphlet and later in his book, *Servant Leadership*,[6] he illustrates the concept with a German tale about a group of important men who went on a long journey into the wilderness, accompanied by a servant. They got lost and fell into deep trouble. The servant was particularly helpful and became the accepted leader of the group. They came to trust him because he demonstrated attributes of behavior that helped them get out of trouble. So their servant became their leader and the others became his constituents.

"Servant leadership" is becoming part of the language. Walter Kiechel III wrote in *Fortune* that the two words "servant leadership" are "a juxtaposition of apparent opposites meant to startle the seeker after wisdom into new insight: The leader exists to serve those whom he nominally leads, those who supposedly follow him."[7]

Certainly having the servant-leadership viewpoint helps any leader, particularly the chief executive; he or she focuses on company performance and the needs of constituents rather than his or her own performance or image. The chief executive knows that he or she will get credit for good corporate performance as well as blame for poor performance. So the chief who is a leader can plunge wholeheartedly into leading other company leaders in improving overall company performance, knowing that chief executive performance is always being carefully watched by everyone in the company.

Any chief executive seeking to be a leader will avoid the behavior of the chief executive depicted in the best-selling *Barbarians at the Gate* (Harper & Row, 1990). The book depicts the corporate life of the then chief executive of RJR Nabisco. The company's fleet of corporate jets was used freely for his own personal enjoyment, as well as the many golf clubs to which he belonged at company expense. His social life was supported by the planes, clubs, and corporate conferences, all paid for by the company.

That chief executive may have been "king" of the small set of chief executives who behave similarly and are sometimes referred to as "United States royalty." But no true leader will choose to play "the CEO game." The example he or she would set within the company would be devastating, as was the example set by the RJR Nabisco chief executive.

The genuine leader also steers away from ostentatious corporate headquarters. I well remember the beginning of the trend of moving corporate headquarters from New York City to the suburbs and nearby Connecticut to escape the city's higher taxes. As one corporation followed another, the headquarters became increasingly elaborate. One building is called the "Taj Mahal"; another has museum-quality statuary on the grounds. And so it is refreshing to read, as I write, that IBM, which was a part of that trend, is now joining a reverse trend. It has put up for sale its present headquarters office in Armonk, New York, a structure designed by prestigious architects, built on a hill overlooking landscaped grounds.

The senior vice president of human resources and administration told the *New York Times:*

> Our view of corporate headquarters is that there should be as little of it as possible. . . . There are no sacred cows here anymore, and that includes Armonk. . . . There will have to be someplace for [Chairman] Lou Gerstner, me and a few other people to sit, but there's nothing that says it has to be in Armonk. . . . The big building on the hill is more and more a thing of the past.[8]

This tells us something about the direction that the present American revolution in managing is taking. It also points up one of the differences between leaders and managers: Successful leaders are as unassuming in the surroundings they create—or tolerate—as they are in their behavior.

Casualness and informality contribute to a leadership culture. In some successful high-tech companies, everyone dresses and behaves informally; it's integral to the company culture. At General Electric, this is increasingly the pattern.

I seriously suggest that everyone in a company be on a first-name basis. It may seem corny but it helps drive out vestiges of past hierarchy. I was slow in moving this custom along in McKinsey, but it has improved our cohesiveness and bonding significantly. Now when I talk on the phone to a colleague I have never met, we are on a first-name basis. It reinforces our one-firm concept.

Which brings me to two Ian MacGregors. On a visit to our London office, I was provided with a car and driver to call on clients. On the way to the Coal Board to see the unassuming leader, Sir Ian MacGregor, I learned that the driver's name was also Ian MacGregor. After our visit, I asked Sir Ian if he would come down to the car to meet the other Ian, which he was delighted to do. When I introduced them, Sir Ian, characteristically, made an amusing remark that put the driver completely at ease. The next morning Ian, the driver, said he had told his wife about the meeting. And he added, "She'll never look on me the same!"

I'm sure that other examples of unassuming leaders will come readily to the minds of chief executives who think of themselves as chief servants of their companies, but let me add a few more:

- Unassuming leaders surprise visitors and company people with their offices: pleasant, inviting, and functional, but completely unostentatious in either size or decor. And they leave their desks to sit with visitors.

- Four-star general Norman Schwarzkopf, commander of Operation Desert Storm, was offered a villa by the Saudis but he chose instead a small room tucked away behind his office.[9]

- I know several executives who have "chairman" on their business cards and letterhead but not "chief executive officer," even though they hold both titles.

- I know two chief executives who often stand in line at headquarters cafeterias and then join a group at one of the general tables.

- The McKinsey research on excellent companies, which ultimately became *In Search of Excellence,*[10] found that unassuming executives "walk around" rather than holding all meetings in their own offices.

If all company leaders have an unassuming manner—with the casualness and informality that it produces—the resulting behaviors of people will fit naturally into a leadership culture.

Leaders Listen. Listening may seem like an unimportant activity, but my experience convinces me that quite the reverse is true. In a survey for a major manufacturing plant in the Chicago area, one of the participants said: "Frankly, I had never thought of listening as an important subject by itself. But now that I am aware of it, I think that perhaps 80% of my work depends on my listening to someone, or on someone else listening to me."[11]

I have observed that a high proportion of CEOs in command companies don't listen very well. They may even turn off people who have valuable information to provide; and one turn-off may discourage the person from coming forward the next time with even more valuable information.

In fact, chief executives of command companies are generally such poor listeners that they can signal their change to leading by simply beginning to listen. The shift from telling to listening can be startling to subordinates—and I guarantee will be well received by them. Indeed, at first, the listening will be flattering to subordinates. And emerging leaders will be surprised by how much of importance they will learn.

The late Charles Mortimer, chairman of General Foods, was a fine listening chief executive. He often told me things he had learned by listening, and on which he was taking action. Indeed, Charlie was unusual: He was openly trying to improve his own performance. We'll hear more about him later.

In meetings, I have observed that chief executives often close off opportunities to learn by expressing their own views too early in the discussion. I know one brilliant chief executive of an overseas world-class company who does this constantly. His colleagues have concluded that he is subconsciously showing off his brilliance. But that habit, together with the awe in which he is held, cuts him off from important facts and useful opinions.

Active listening helps assure the other person that he or she is being heard and understood. That not only involves paying close attention, but also asking brief, nonleading questions. These convey interest and understanding without necessarily implying agreement.

But a word of caution. Listening customs vary around the world. One American executive I know went to England to negotiate an alliance. He was successful, but the affiliation proved to be worthless. His rueful afterthought: "I wish I had known then that when most Britons nod their heads, it means 'I understand you,' not 'I agree with you.' "

Because the global economy has become a reality, this is an episode for Americans to bear in mind. For even at this late date, American executives, compared with Europeans, are still provincial. Most Americans start out with no second language, whereas educated Europeans know three or four. Also, young Europeans travel to learn languages, and they learn something of the cultures of the other countries at the same time.

When McKinsey began expanding around the world, I gave every American consultant who moved to another country a copy of *The*

Silent Language by Edward T. Hall (Doubleday, 1959). The title gives most of the message. The book deals with cultures and customs: attitudes toward punctuality, dress, body language (which my friend who went to Britain did not know), and other important behaviors that communicate silently. The book is still available in paperback although, disappointingly, it has not been updated. Still, the message the title brings is forever.

Perhaps the importance of listening as an attribute will have greater impact on learning leadership if I quote the importance it played in the election, by *Fortune* in 1994, of six new members of the National Business Hall of Fame, each of whom was "blessed as much with forehearing as foresight."

> Of all the skills of leadership, listening is one of the most valuable—and one of the least understood. Most captains of industry listen only sometimes, and they remain ordinary leaders. But a few, the great ones, never stop listening. They are hear-aholics, ever alert, bending their ears while they work and while they play, while they eat and while they sleep. They listen to advisers, to customers, to inner voices, to enemies, to the wind. That's how they get word before anyone else of unseen problems and opportunities.[12]

This seemingly simple attribute—along with open-mindedness—can have enormous importance to any company and contribute to competitive advantage for any company.

A Leader Is Open-Minded. Over the years, I have encountered a high proportion of chief executives whose minds were closed, or if not closed were only slightly ajar. As a consultant, I admit to being sensitive to this failing: What's the use of hiring consultants if your mind is closed even to considering their findings and recommendations?

I've thought a lot about why so many chief executives are not more open-minded, and I lay much of the blame on the command-and-control system. The all-powerful chief executive sits at the top, managing mostly from there. People don't question chief executives much, and they seldom disagree with them. So CEOs become self-believers and commanders of others. That's pretty heady stuff, and it feeds on itself.

Self-assurance can be a plus, but excessive self-assurance leads to egotism and even arrogance; it certainly closes minds. I've seen it happen.

The leader may get an idea—for example, an acquisition: Quaker Oats buying Snapple—and the leader (e.g., the CEO) has an open mind about the good and bad features of the acquisition. On the other hand, a CEO in a command company might get an idea about an acquisition and not want any negative information about it—and if the CEO does not have a reputation for being open-minded, people in the company would likely not come forward with negative information. Whereas a leader would be known to have an open mind, so people would feel free to come forward with both positive and negative information.

The difference between a leadership and a command company can be very great indeed, because in a hierarchical situation, people who have concerns about reactions against themselves would simply not put forward negative information. When in doubt, people in a command company are likely to keep still and not give bosses negative information.

Any leader with an open mind makes better judgments, learns more of what he or she needs to know, and establishes more positive relations with subordinates and constituents. Again, the willingness to listen with a mind that is eager to acquire new knowledge and insights promotes the free, two-way flow of ideas, information, and opinions between leaders and their constituents (which is the heart of leadership).

In a leadership company—without hierarchy and with people free to speak their minds about company performance and how to improve it—people can be more productive. Consider the great competitive advantage to a company of having an open-minded chief executive as a leader and other open-minded leaders positioned throughout the company, all ready to receive and consider ideas and put them to work if their judgments stamp them as useful.

Let me give a McKinsey example. One of our people responsibilities is maintaining a nonhierarchical working atmosphere throughout the firm, so that anybody can talk freely with anybody else—and disagree with anybody—without having to worry about any consequences. While I was managing director I followed this practice: When visiting offices, I talked individually with associates, including new associates. I learned a great deal that was worthwhile.

On a visit to our Swiss office in Geneva in April 1965, two new Swiss associates asked to meet with me. Their question: "Do you want to have a practice in Switzerland?" Yes, I told them, that's why we have this office. Then they both told me that we would not be able to develop a broad practice in Geneva, or from Geneva. Their reasons: First, the area had no significant banks or manufacturing companies; second, we had already served several of the international organizations located in Geneva and the European headquarters of several American companies located there; and third, travel from Geneva was so difficult that Swiss nationals would be reluctant to join the office.

They went on to tell me why Zurich was the better location, as well as the better place from which to travel throughout Europe and overseas. I told them their views seemed persuasive on all counts. I suggested they work with the office manager, associates, and any others they wished in order to prepare a report for the managing committee recommending that we change office locations. This report should include a budget for dealing with office transfer costs and the residence costs of moving our people.

Two months later I received an excellent report, documenting all issues and giving a realistic budget. The report was circulated not only to the managing committee but to all European partners, who were asked for comments. The managing committee approved the move; an announcement was sent to the consulting staffs in all offices, which included the names of the two associates whose advice had initiated the move.

By my next visit to Switzerland in April 1966—this time to Zurich—the move had been completed. Geneva had been closed; the Zurich office had been leased and furnished; all Geneva residences had been disposed of and new ones found in Zurich. And all were under budget. As soon as I came into the new office I sought out the two associates and asked them what they thought now. "Now," they said, "we'll have a Swiss practice." And we have.

As constituents come to learn that their leader does indeed listen with an open mind, they'll gain confidence in offering their opinions and in engaging in those full, free exchanges of thought that can turn into useful brainstorming sessions. Even the small ideas that emerge can be useful to the leader, and sometimes they can be developed into ideas of real importance. The leader can easily control the time devoted to such sessions: Constituents themselves will sense when the leader needs or wants to end the discussion and get on with other business.

It isn't hard to keep an open mind once you accept its great value. However, for anyone who is learning to be open-minded and who wishes to gain a reputation for being so, the following guidelines may help: "Never say no immediately." Of course you have to give a response of some sort, and it should be "I'll get back to you." Then, after taking time for thought, at least overnight, the decision in all likelihood will be a better one for not having been made on the spot. But whatever the decision, don't fail to get back to those to whom you've promised to respond. Particularly, be meticulous in responding to anything submitted in writing.

Sensitivity to People. Most leadership scholars call this attribute "skill in dealing with people." To me that smacks of managing or even manipulating people, as though the leader should develop mechanical approaches or a studied synthetic "style" for dealing with people. Moreover, treating this attribute as a *skill* focuses the mind of the leader inwardly, in a self-centered way, instead of outwardly on helping or persuading constituents.

The reality is that the leader can't motivate or persuade constituents, or others, effectively without having some sense of what's on their minds. So unless constituents, or others, are always forthcoming about what is on their minds (which is unrealistic to expect), the leader must try to discern what they're thinking and feeling. That's why I prefer to call this important attribute "sensitivity to people."

Based on my experience, I believe a leader can develop competence in guessing what's on people's minds. Once my late partner, Zip

Reilley, had convinced me to give up commanding and try persuading, I knew that I could persuade people better if I guessed what was going on inside them. It seemed to me, however, that I had to start paying attention to everyone I dealt with every day.

By this I mean I had to stop taking them for granted and exercise insights, intuition, perception, empathy—or some combination of these in the guesswork of trying to find out what was on their minds. That's the "soft" approach, and eventually I got the hang of it. I suggest that nearly anyone with the will to lead can do the same.

There is also the "hard" approach of inferring their thoughts from the facts and specific information you have about them. Try both the "soft" and "hard." The way you learn to gain insights from people is by paying attention to them and trying to guess what's on their minds.

There is a stereotype that women have more intuition than men. My own experience confirms the stereotype. In McKinsey we work extensively with teams made up of our own people or combined with client people. I have observed that when I have worked for some time with an all-male team and then add a woman, the team becomes more imaginative, has more and better ideas, and is more sensitive to what's on the minds of client people. It is well to keep this in mind in making up leadership teams.

Sensitivity to people also means that leaders are sensitive to their feelings. Leaders are polite, considerate, understanding, and careful that what they say to someone is not dispiriting unless criticism is intended. Leaders, especially chief executives, must be careful not to be overheard discussing someone's job performance with another person. There's nothing new in that but it's frequently overlooked.

Since sensitivity to people and to situations calls for using some form of imagination, this is a good place to make an assertion I can't prove: I believe that most people's imaginations can be expanded on the job.

The dictionary says (roughly) that imagination is the creative ability to form a mental image of something not present in the senses. Clearly that ability is valuable to a leader. My assertion is that someone who has imagination can expand it by trying to form mental images that the person believes in sufficiently to act on them.

For example, I began thinking about McKinsey's becoming an international firm after reading Wendell L. Willkie's book *One World* (1943), where he wrote that ". . . [m]en and women all over the world are . . . beginning to know that men's welfare throughout the world is interdependent."[13] After deliberating on that "mental image" a long time, McKinsey acted on it.

Sensitivity to Situations. Situations are created by people and must be dealt with by people. Any company leader who is called on to resolve a dispute or disagreement must combine a careful analysis of the facts with an acute sensitivity to the feelings and attitudes of the people involved.

Take the case of a large food manufacturing conglomerate that developed a strategy of acquiring other food companies to increase share of market and profits. A small task force scoured the country for several years for acquisition candidates. Finally, a fast-food chain became available. The task force studied the candidate company carefully and recommended to the president and chief operating officer that it be acquired.

The acquisition was made. After several years, however, poor results created a drag on the conglomerate's profits. On closer examination, the conglomerate's chief executive realized that a fast-food chain was an entirely different type of business from that of a food manufacturer. Key factors for success were proper selection of sites and selection and training of people to make and serve the products—as contrasted with manufacturing products in volume, followed by effective packaging, distribution, advertising, and promotion. The conglomerate sold the fast-food chain (ironically, to another food manufacturer) and took a large charge against earnings. The president was fired.

This disaster could have been avoided by a more searching, sensitive, and intuitive investigation by the people involved. In that conglomerate, managed by command and control, members of the task force expected a successful outcome to mean advancements for them—and the president expected the acquisition to clinch his promotion to chairman. Thus the objectivity of the task force and the president were undermined by personal ambitions. And poor judgment by the president cost him his job. He failed to sense intuitively that he should have challenged the task force's objectivity more rigorously before authorizing the acquisition. But the chief executive was really the one at fault.

(Or it might have been the fault of the company's corporate governance. See Chapter 9.)

Initiative, Initiative, Initiative. Initiative is one of the most important attributes of every leader. It is also easy to learn: Just think a bit, use judgment, and *act*. The important thing is to keep alert for opportunities.

American chief executives seldom lack initiative, however, because their boards wouldn't have elected them if they felt the candidate lacked initiative. Every board knows that the chief executive has responsibility for getting things going and keeping them going. Even so, command-and-control managing inhibits initiative, especially down the line.

But consider the dynamics of a leadership company run with a network of leaders: All leaders stationed strategically throughout the company are alert to taking initiatives at every opportunity. And constituents as well as leaders can suggest initiatives.

In a seminar on managing that I organized at the Salzburg Seminar in American Studies, my late friend Bob Greenleaf attended as a faculty member. In a lecture, Bob said, "Nothing in this world happens except at the initiative of a single person." Under scrutiny this observation stands up well. It points up the action opportunities open to every leader and constituent in a leadership company, thus making an important contribution to competitive advantage.

And when I think about it, serving clients in the law and advising clients on running a business both call for continuous initiative. Because clients can't tell us what to do to serve them, we must know and decide what to do in developing our recommendations. Even then, we must exercise still more initiative in persuading client people to act on our recommendations. Continuous initiative will often be needed in a business.

I think I need not go further to establish the importance of initiative in leading.

Good Judgment. John Gardner gives this definition of judgment, of which every leader would do well to memorize the first sentence:

> *Judgment is the ability to combine hard data, questionable data and intuitive guesses to arrive at a conclusion that events prove to be correct.* [Emphasis added.] Judgment-in-action includes effective problem solving, the design of strategies, the setting of priorities and intuitive as well as rational judgments. Most important, perhaps, it includes the capacity to appraise the potentialities of coworkers and opponents.[14]

Boards of directors, of course, make one of their most important decisions when they elect their chief executives on the basis of board members' collective judgment. Incoming chief executives can always be sure that their boards have confidence in their judgment, because the board will have considered the person's judgment as one of the most important selection criteria. Thereafter, in setting strategic priorities and in making those decisions of greatest importance to the company, the chief executive must first make the final judgment before asking for the board's approval.

But often there are no hard data for such decisions; they must be based largely on questionable data and intuitive guesses. To a lesser degree this is true for other leaders throughout the company.

In running companies there is no shortage of bad judgment. For example, shortly after a leveraged buyout, the chief executive of R. H. Macy & Company decided to buy two additional department store chains. The board approved his decision, although one director was strongly opposed. After Macy took Chapter 11 bankruptcy, knowledgeable observers concluded that if the debt for the two additional chains had not been added, the company could have met its heavy debt service.[15] Perhaps the greed of the 1980s undermined good judgment, or maybe it was executive pride in wanting to head a larger company.

Following fads in running companies often reflects bad judgment.

Adopting Japanese manufacturing ideas provides an example. The *Wall Street Journal* article on the subject began this way:

> Some American manufacturers are discarding billions of dollars of investment they made in the 1980s to adopt Japanese manufacturing ideas.
>
> They haven't decided that the Japanese systems don't work. Rather, they realize that some of those systems, however useful in lifting productivity in Japan, haven't achieved much in their own plants.[16]

I can think of many cases of bad judgment in making acquisitions of new types of businesses to shore up weak earnings (and weak management) in the core business. (Westinghouse, for example, bought furniture companies.) Acquiring insurance companies and other financial institutions were popular mistakes that are still being undone.

In January 1994, in a statement at the time of laying off 3,400 employees, Michael H. Jordan—then the new chief executive of Westinghouse brought in from outside—said that most of the company's debt related to bad investments in financial services.[17] Of course, hindsight is easy—but too many acquisitions are based simply on the chief executive's wish to make the company larger, a prime cause of bad judgment.

In my opinion, the chief executive of a leadership company is more likely to make good judgments than the chief of a command-and-control company, simply because constituents—recognizing the leader's open-mindedness and willingness to listen—will be more willing to volunteer their candid opinions.

I also believe that multiple first-among-equals leaders in a leadership company will make decisions of a consistently higher quality because many leaders and their constituents will be involved in much of the decision making. The added judgments may determine what additional data and information should be gathered and who else, in addition to direct constituents, should be consulted in the decision.

People whose judgments have been tested and usually found to be sound are an invaluable resource. We had such a McKinsey partner who, I believe, could be found or replicated in any business to great advantage: Everett Smith (now deceased), one of our early partners. Often when, as managing partner, I suggested an important action, Everett opposed it until we made changes.

At first I was irritated, but then I found that Ev's judgment was nearly always correct, combining hard data and intuitive guesses. Then I observed that other partners also recognized his sound judgments. I came to regard his judgment as a valuable resource, especially when the issue was important.

For instance, having thought for some time about McKinsey's becoming an international firm, I decided in the early 1950s that it was time to get serious about expanding internationally. After careful study, most partners favored the idea, but Ev did not, mainly because it was risky and we still had many opportunities in the United States.

I decided immediately that we had to convince Ev. Under our policy, opening a new office requires persuading partners and associates (and their families) to move—this time overseas. I sensed that most would not be willing to go unless there was unanimous agreement, which really meant that Ev had to be in favor.

But Ev kept raising obstacles; he gave sound enough reasons that had to be met. We agreed we had to follow our U.S. strategy, serve the same calibre of clients, and recruit the same calibre of associates. Finally, Ev put forth the requirement that we should not go overseas until we had a major European client. Everyone agreed, but to me it looked like a long delay.

To our great surprise it was only a few months before Royal Dutch/ Shell decided to retain an American consulting firm to study its whole business, provided the firm first studied (to Shell's satisfaction) its largest operating subsidiary, which was in Caracas, Venezuela. We agreed, of course, and it worked out well. Everyone I asked moved for at least a few years; one who moved for two years actually stayed through to retirement.

Luck was with us, but there is no telling what might have happened had we not responded to Ev's requirements. (When Ev was retiring I told him again what great contributions his good judgment had made to the firm.)

Any company can strengthen the quality of its decision making by seeking out people with good judgment among its network of leaders. Moreover, in a leadership company—where constituents can speak up—their judgments, too, can make important contributions.

Broad-Mindedness. My dictionary defines the word "broad-minded" as "tolerant of varied views" and "inclined to condone minor departures from conventional behavior." This attribute, of course, is closely related to being open-minded, adaptable, and flexible. Other aspects of broad-mindedness are being undisturbed by little things, willing to overlook small errors, and easy to talk with. Leaders are somehow thought of as being broad-minded or broad-gauged.

This is probably as good a place as any to bring up sense of humor. It's hardly an attribute, but it can serve everybody well. A leader with a sense of humor will certainly get along better with everyone, and any leader who has a sense of humor should nourish it constantly and be thankful for having it.

Flexibility and Adaptability. Flexibility and adaptability go hand in hand with open-minded listening. The chief executive and other leaders thereby show their readiness to consider change and their willingness to make changes when most agree they are needed.

When competitive circumstances call for change, I'm convinced a leadership company will always be more ready for it. Beginning with the chief executive, all leaders will keep their minds open and alert to the need for continuous improvement in all segments of the enterprise. In doing so, they will learn how to spot the need for change faster, initiate change, and adapt to it.

The Capacity to Make Sound and Timely Decisions. A sound (i.e., high-quality) decision by an individual chief executive in a command company depends largely on his or her ability to think and to seek advice from others. In a leadership company, there will be fewer individual decisions, even by the chief executive. Most decisions will be checked by others, at the CEO's request or the initiative of others. In fact, in a leadership company all decisions should be of higher quality because so many people are free to speak up and to disagree.

But now is the time to tell you about the help that Charlie Mortimer gave me when he was chairman of General Foods. In one of our sessions, he gave me a pamphlet by Robert Rawls entitled *Time Out for Mental Digestion* (now long out of print, but the title gives the message). Charlie told me that he followed the message faithfully and found that his decision making improved substantially. Ever since then, I've followed it too, and with surprising success. Perhaps it will work for others.

The primary words are "mental digestion"; they have more meaning for me than the old phrase "mulling it over." "Mulling" connotes turning over the same thought, whereas "mental digestion" puts the original thought out of mind for a time. Mental digestion, at least overnight, almost always brings new options from which to choose. For something of real importance, however, overnight will usually not be enough time out for new options to develop. Then I may wait a week or two to decide whether the decision or action will still be timely; again, I put the thought out of mind and again new options come to mind each time I go back to it. That's the "mental digestion."

This concept may not work for you, but it has for me, even in writing this book. I'm sure my overall decision making improved after Charlie gave me the pamphlet and emphasized that it had worked for him.

All leaders—particularly the chief executive—must recognize that the speed as well as the quality of their decisions will set an example for others. I've observed a number of busy chief executives who appear to be indecisive but are not. They can make up their minds all right, but they simply do not realize that delaying the decisions (or failing to communicate the decisions) not only erodes effective performance, but also irritates those waiting for decisions. They could correct this simply by setting priorities and asking their assistants to remind them to follow up.

Some make decisions too quickly. One chief executive I worked with surprised me with his consistently rapid-fire decision making. When we explored this pattern, it turned out that he had been a baseball umpire in college and had carried the habit over into business.

Once he was aware of the reason, it was easy for him to slow down—and the quality of his decisions went up.

In a leadership company, it might not have taken an outsider (me) to help that executive improve his decision making. In a leadership culture, people are more likely to help each other learn how to decide, as well as how to do anything else so as to improve on their individual, as well as company, performance. Competition among individuals to get ahead will likely be replaced by support of people to help each other improve company performance.

The Capacity to Motivate. John Gardner says it well: ". . . More than any other attribute, this is close to the heart of the popular conception of leadership—the capacity to move people to action, to communicate persuasively, to strengthen the confidence of followers. . . ."[18]

Group motivation is part of the mystique and power of leadership. Much of that power comes from motivating people through group goals tied to the good of the enterprise: for example, participating in increasing long-term growth, competing more successfully in the global economy, making the company more flexible or a more enjoyable place to work, or simply achieving the company's mission for satisfying the customer.

If leaders can sense what constituents are feeling and thinking, they can readily determine through everyday experience what will motivate them to achieve the goals they have in common.

Too often, in so-called modern managing, motivations take the form of monetary rewards for the individual, or promises to the individual for advancement within the company. Both are characteristic of command-and-control managing that should not be carried over into a leadership company.

In a leadership company, people will be motivated by example and the satisfaction they get daily from making valuable contributions to the company, and from being treated fairly, with dignity and consideration.

These are motivations they can take home every day. And since everyone should participate in profit sharing and be owners of stock, they will have financial incentives as well.

Longer term, people in a leadership company derive satisfaction from being involved in work which produces products or services that customers buy with increasing satisfaction. And, for everyone, simply belonging to a leadership company will be satisfying in itself.

A Sense of Urgency. One of the ways currently advocated for improving the command system is to use time (that is, speed) to provide a competitive edge: Get out new products on time, deliver orders on time, get things done faster than competitors. All are useful practices if done without adversely affecting quality.

Early in my McKinsey career, I observed that many outstanding companies had a sense of urgency underlying everything they did—a refreshing difference from companies where every response is either slow or erratic. I also noticed that invariably the chief executive set the urgency pace, which was promptly followed throughout the company.

We have built a sense of urgency into McKinsey, and it has worked well in serving clients, in facilitating our growth, and in many other ways. The freedom of partners to check other partners usually prevents undue speed. (I, for example, recommended opening an office in Tokyo well before my partners would agree.)

When a sense of urgency has spread throughout a company, it can make a substantial difference in both effectiveness and efficiency, and it is easier to speed up activities further when necessary. Good judgment usually provides a sensible definition of how much urgency is necessary in a particular situation. Moreover, people like to work in a company where "things happen." A sense of urgency is a useful ingredient in a leadership culture.

And a sense of urgency is easy to establish in a leadership company. With the chief executive setting an example, every leader throughout the company can, in turn, set an example for his or her constituents.

Getting Started

Whether or not the ultimate plan is to convert the business to a leadership company, I suggest that the CEO take immediate steps to become a leader. No matter how the company is run now, this change—from managing to leading—will, I am sure, increase the CEO's effectiveness in running the total business.

The CEO will already have the trust of the board—and probably of his or her direct reports. The challenge will be to convince bosses throughout the company that they can trust the CEO. To achieve this trust and become leaders, some CEOs may need only become more consistent in their present behavior; others may find that they will have to undergo a major behavioral overhaul, a prospect that may prove too daunting for them to undertake.

My experience has been that most CEOs will fall in between these two extremes. They will be natural learners and eager to try what works. In this instance, I'm convinced that what works in learning to lead will be to expend effort in three areas: learning to listen to people "actively" with an open mind, demonstrating high-precision truthfulness in all dealings, and becoming unassuming and approachable in behavior. Combined, these basic changes in a CEO's behavior are likely to be so surprising to constituents that they will almost immediately respond favorably.

In making the decision whether to become a leader immediately, I suggest that the CEO re-read the early pages of this chapter about becoming a leader—especially the sections about trustworthiness, listening, and open-mindedness. Then as the CEO learns, more attributes can be added to the learning list.

There is another plus: As the CEO changes behavior in these ways, he or she will be able to judge the difficulties that others may have in changing their behaviors to become leaders.

Four Fundamental Responsibilities of Company Leaders

N O MATTER WHERE they are located in the business, executives who want to become true leaders must be prepared to commit themselves to learning four responsibilities that are central to developing mutual trust and common interests with their constituents.

1. Treating Constituents with Respect

Leaders throughout the company have the responsibility for treating all constituents (their own and others') as unique and valued individuals. That means they must assume the best about people rather than the worst, and act in the belief that most people who are treated fairly and considerately will perform whatever work they are doing more effectively and efficiently. In fact, a leadership culture creates the right environment for people to enjoy their work.

I have observed a few command companies whose chief executives were so considerate of people that almost everyone in the company behaved as though they were constituents of the chief executive.

I remember well my late friend Paul L. Davies, chairman of Food Machinery Company (now FMC Corporation), with whom I worked closely during World War II. Paul had such a high-precision level of truthfulness that everyone trusted him implicitly. He was an intent listener, fair, considerate, respectful, and sensitive to people's feelings. People, in turn, followed his example. He persuaded, never ordered. He was a true leader. Indeed, Paul had nearly all the attributes discussed in the previous chapter. (Under his leadership, his small machinery company expanded into a Fortune 500 corporation, with successor chief executives developed from within.)

Treating people with respect raises a question about the present practice of calling them "human resources," which I personally dislike. The word "resources" connotes inanimate objects, such as steel, rubber, and wood. People are human beings who would, I believe, prefer to be called "individuals" or just plain "people," and be treated that way. However, in recent years, the title "Director of Personnel" has been replaced by "Vice President, Human Resources." Chief executives of outstanding companies speak of their people proudly in their annual reports and yet have officers for "human resources."

Since everything that goes on in a company happens because of decisions and actions taken by people, these important people are more likely to be treated with consideration, fairness, and respect if they are not called, or regarded, as "human resources." A few companies are using the title "Vice President for [not of] People." I think that is a better motivator; but some companies may improve on that.

2. Developing Constituent Self-Confidence and Self-Esteem

Implicit in command-and-control managing is the assumption that fear is a positive motivator. And, sadly, over the years, I have witnessed the mass destruction of self-confidence and self-esteem by bosses who make mean and snide criticisms to their subordinates about their job performance—and, worse still, in the presence of others. They ignore the obvious: subordinates' inherent fear or anxiety derived from the plain fact that the boss controls their compensation, advancement, and standing in the company.

A constituent cannot be effective—or take personal satisfaction in a job—if he or she lacks self-confidence. "Loss of confidence," says Gardner, "brings images of defeat and failure, helplessness, even self-contempt. Among the direct consequences are an incapacity to summon energy in behalf of purposeful effort, an unwillingness to take risks, and a fatal timidity when the moment of opportunity breaks."[1]

This need not be. Confidence can easily be developed even in people who are new to the organization, simply by searching for opportunities to involve them in improving company performance early, and by offering genuine praise for the good work they do. Obviously, genuine praise for good work builds confidence in people of any tenure, as does telling others about a person's good work.

Therefore, every leader has the important responsibility for developing self-confidence and self-esteem in constituents and for making them feel good about themselves. Here's what one vice president of a very large command company told me about an unassuming chief executive who is a real leader: "I never leave his office without feeling good—not even when he turns me down on something or criticizes me. But he never tries to show me up or put me down. Everyone around here feels that same way, but he is decisive and tough when he has to be." That chief executive recognized the importance of building self-esteem and self-confidence in people.

Every leader should recognize the importance of building self-confidence and self-esteem in his or her constituents and making them feel good about themselves. I learned that from Gilbert Clee, one of my partners in McKinsey who died early from cancer. I saw the outstanding performances of associates who were his constituents, not his subordinates, and the satisfaction they got from working with him. Gil would get the team together at the outset, tell them how important the institution of business is, how worthwhile our work is in improving client performance, and how we would help clients with their work. So they started with a feeling of self-confidence; and Gil praised them when their work deserved it. Not only constituents followed his example; other partners did as well. I know I did.

Along with self-confidence, there is self-esteem. We are more likely to have self-esteem when we feel that our lives have meaning and that what we do for a living is regarded by others as worthwhile. Today, business is recognized as both worthwhile and important. But this was not always so. You will recall Dean Pound's negative reaction in the late 1920s when I told him I was going to Harvard Business School.

But now business is recognized as largely determining the level of employment and every nation's standard of living. (Indeed, in the recession of 1989–92, television showed workers marching in the streets carrying signs and shouting, "We want jobs!") Business as an institution is clearly recognized as worthwhile and is right up there with the professions in choosing a career. However, as I have observed, people who work for command-and-control businesses cannot always count on being treated as well as they should be, and so they shy away from large corporations.

In the future, I believe that working in a leadership company will be considered to be as prestigious as working in the professions, and more worthwhile than working in a command-and-control company. There are two reasons: First, people will be treated with greater fairness and consideration. Second, they will be more deeply involved in improving company performance and ensuring its future success, which will give them greater personal satisfaction in their work. Altogether, working in a leadership company with people who create an attractive culture will make the company a desirable and even noble place to work.

Leaders should also serve as examples of commitment and enthusiasm, which should lift the spirits of constituents. If they are to make superior contributions to company performance, all constituents need continual reinforcement of their self-confidence and self-esteem. All leaders (especially the chief executive) need to increase their constituents' confidence and lift their spirits. Consider the strength of the company when a network of confident leaders is stationed throughout.

3. Developing Constituents

Among the toasts at Sir Ian MacGregor's 80th birthday party that I attended in New York in 1992, four members of the small party of colleagues and close friends rose to express their appreciation for Ian's role in developing their careers at AMAX, where they then served as officers. AMAX is where Ian spent the last years of his impressive American career before he moved back to the United Kingdom, where he was appointed head of the British Steel Corporation and the Coal Board by Prime Minister Thatcher. He was knighted for this.

At breakfast with Ian the next morning, I told him he must have been greatly pleased by the praise of his former colleagues. My longtime friend typically replied, "That's not so great. Every leader is supposed to develop his people."

All leaders are, indeed, responsible to their companies and to their people for developing the potential of their constituents and for bringing along new generations of leaders from these constituents. But true leaders, such as Sir Ian, know it and do it gracefully and without fanfare.

I have observed that most successful chief executives pay careful attention to developing their successors, and those who don't are quite rightly sharply criticized for not doing so. Shell and General Electric give particular attention to this CEO responsibility, as does DuPont. (At one time in the DuPont Company, there were so many CEO candidates that they were quietly referred to as "cardinals" or "red hats.") Consider, then, the benefits that can accrue to a leadership company when leaders stationed strategically throughout the company all discharge their responsibility for developing their constituents and future leaders.

Gardner says, "If a leader has the will to develop people, there is no great mystery in how to do it. Experts have written extensively on the subject: Bring them in on decisions. Delegate. Feed them responsibility. Stretch them. And change their assignments periodically."[2] At the heart of it all, of course, is the basic mindset of really wanting to help other people succeed. That is the mindset of a leader.

4. Making Constituents Stakeholders

All leaders must give their constituents the feeling that they have a real stake (or part) in the company's present performance and future success. The form of the stake will vary by industry, company, division—but it must be real.

Next, they must help constituents understand the business: not just their immediate part of it, but the business as a whole, beginning with its purpose, key factors for success, culture, ways competition can be dealt with, and how profits are earned.

Only then will constituents come to feel that their stake is real and that they can feel free to offer opinions and ideas that go beyond their own job (or team) responsibilities. Take, for example, the Argentinian employee of Levi Strauss & Company, the jeans people, who suggested a new type of casual clothing (later named Dockers) that now has sales of more than $1 billion a year.

In a leadership company leaders and their constituents at every level will be motivated by their stakeholding to increase productivity by contributing valuable ideas to increase revenue or decrease costs anywhere in the company.

Leaders must seize every opportunity for convincing constituents that their contributions are real and valued. This should not be difficult because constituents will be motivated to work with their leaders in achieving the common goals of their leadership teams, as well as the goals of the whole company. And their work will be even more effective if all leaders and constituents have an understanding of the business as a whole.

I have noticed that whenever I meet or talk with a leader, his or her first reaction is something positive.

Leaders in a company should react positively when they first meet or get together with their colleagues: That is a good beginning for building self-confidence and self-esteem. A leader always makes a positive impression. People should look forward to seeing a leader.

FIVE

Leadership Design: Replacing Structure

W HEN A COMMAND-AND-CONTROL COMPANY is reorganized, decisions are made about what positions are needed and who will report to whom; that provides an organization chart to guide people in exercising and following authority. In a leadership company, decisions must be made about what leaders and what leadership teams are required to run the company most effectively. While leaders will not "report" to one another, their activities must be coordinated—that is, they must have a leadership design to guide them.

Some companies may find the key design factors I suggest useful; some may develop others that will fit their particular needs better. Anyway, this cockshy requires experimentation and innovation. So I offer half a dozen design factors for consideration—perhaps *study* is more accurate.

Treating the Business as a Whole—Integration

Shortly after I joined James O. McKinsey and Company in 1933, I was given what the firm called *The General Survey Outline* (GSO), a 20-page outline of how to study a manufacturing company. It opened with "Outlook for the Industry," moved on to "Competitive Position of the Company," and concluded with an outline for each corporate function.

Its principal message was that every corporation is "a whole," and that we, as consultants, should study it as a whole, because changes affecting one part of the business are likely to affect other parts. So in developing recommendations to clients, we were warned to be careful to consider the business as a whole. That applies also to developing the leadership design as a whole.

The survey concept grew out of *Budgetary Control,* a book that Mac wrote as a professor of management at the University of Chicago, which was published in 1922.[1] Until this seminal book, budgets were developed in pieces (usually by heads of corporate functions) and put together by financial people. Mac's book for making up the budget called for developing an overall operating plan for the year ahead and then putting numbers on it.

Mac pointed out that the chief executive is often the only one who considers the company as a whole (i.e., all functions) in making major decisions. (The current buzzword for wholeness is "holistic.") But in McKinsey we call the CEO approach the "top-management approach" to ensure that we take into consideration all elements (e.g., functions) affecting the decision we are making or the problem we are solving.

Using the top-management approach permits one to consider which parts of the business need to be integrated into the whole. Integration, of course, is the most efficient way of optimizing the piecemeal changes that take place in various parts of the company during the ordinary course of doing business.

Integration is also one of key factors to understanding the kind of leadership design that will best fit the company. In a business that is run by a network of leaders, *all* company leaders—not only the chief executive and a few others—will take the top-management approach and view the business as a whole, that is, they will take decisions and actions from a cross-functional, holistic viewpoint.

In defining integration, Mac's book gives this example: Production executives often contend that the production department should decide what it is equipped to produce, and the sales department should then be instructed to find a market for those products. Sales executives, on the other hand, often contend that it is the function of the production department to serve the sales department and to produce the goods that sales can sell. But Mac says:

> A little consideration will show that neither of these views is correct. *It is the function of each of these departments to serve the business as*

a whole to the end that as much profit as possible may be made. . . .
[Emphasis supplied.] A proper coordination of sales and production,
not only from the viewpoint of quantity, but also from the viewpoint
of profit, is essential. The production equipment should be as flexible
as possible so that changes can be made to meet market conditions,
but a certain amount of standardization is essential to well-regulated
production, and the sales department by proper effort can do much
to increase the sales of those lines which can be produced most
efficiently.[2]

My own definition of integration is "the blending of differing
elements (e.g., functions) to form the most profitable whole." I have
chosen the word "blending" rather than "uniting" or "combining,"
which are sometimes used in defining integration, because I believe
that "blending" best explains the way that integration works.

"Blending" connotes the changes that take place within and among
the differing elements as they are united or combined. Some elements
might not change at all, some might change somewhat, or all elements
might change a little. When you integrate your company, you blend
the elements of running the business by choosing a strategy that will
produce the greatest long-term competitiveness, share of market, and/
or profitability. Thus, integration can be thought of as *a process for
on-line planning of long-term profits.*

Obviously, integration can be accomplished most effectively when
people are objective and make decisions that are best for the *company.*
But in making decisions under the command-and-control system,
people usually weigh personal factors that affect their compensation,
advancement, and standing with the boss. Thus these personal factors,
ever present even though not openly discussed, make it difficult for
people to reach objective integrating decisions.

Understandably, under command-and-control managing, managers of each function are typically reluctant to change their function
for the good of the company. They want to increase their chances for
more compensation, advancement, and better standing, which is why
there are turf battles about authority. Thus integration exposes one

of the major weaknesses of the command system, also one of its strengths: With authority, people's activities can be ordered and controlled.

As we will see later, in a leadership company with hierarchy eliminated, leadership design makes integration much easier and more effective.

Motivating People

In designing a leadership program, leaders must remember that they are not leading the abstract entity we call a "company"; they are leading *people*. Each person differs from every other person in personality, mental and physical makeup, appearance, attitudes, emotions, feelings, and foibles.

Even so, studies show there are common denominators among people: For example, they want to be recognized as individuals and treated with respect, dignity, and fairness. Also, studies show there are some appeals that will motivate most people. So while leaders must recognize the uniqueness of each person, they must also understand human nature well enough to know how to motivate people as members of teams and groups.

In 1960, Douglas McGregor, a professor at Sloan School of Business of Massachusetts Institute of Technology, wrote a groundbreaking book on understanding human nature in a working environment: *The Human Side of Enterprise* (McGraw-Hill). This outstanding book made a scathing attack on command-and-control managing and made the terms Theory X and Theory Y famous. Although quoted widely, the book's concepts have not been put broadly into actual use; otherwise command-and-control managing would have expired long ago.

McGregor's book provides such important guidelines for developing the design for a leadership company that I call on my friend and former McKinsey partner Robert H. Waterman, Jr. (co-author of *In Search of Excellence*) for his summary of Theory X and Theory Y in his recent book *What America Does Right* (W.W. Norton, 1994).

In Bob's view these are the main *negative* tenets of Theory X:

- Most of us have an inherent dislike of work and will avoid it if at all possible.
- We need to be directed, want to avoid responsibility, have relatively little ambition, and want security above all.
- We need, therefore, to be coerced, controlled, directed, and threatened with punishment if we're to put forward adequate effort.

McGregor's own beliefs, which he labeled Theory Y, were the polar opposite (again in Bob's words):

- Putting forth physical and mental effort in work is as natural as play or rest.
- Most humans don't inherently dislike work, though they are often placed in jobs that give them plenty of cause for unhappiness.
- External control and threat of punishment are not the only means for getting us to work.
- Commitment to objectives is directly related to the rewards attached to achieving those objectives; the most important reward: satisfaction of our own ego needs.
- Under favorable conditions, most of us learn not only to accept, but to seek, responsibility.
- The capacity to enact a fairly high degree of imagination, ingenuity, and creativity is widely, not narrowly, distributed in the population.[3]

Thus, McGregor's Theory Y describes the motivations of people who are led instead of commanded. So, more than 30 years later, running a business with a network of leaders provides a way to capitalize more fully on McGregor's Theory Y beliefs.

Two other ways of running a business may also be drawn on, even if it is necessary to retain a few features of command and control. One is based on partnership principles, the other on self-governing principles.

Partnership Principles. A partnership organized under British or U.S. law provides principles that may also contribute to running a leadership business company. In a legal partnership, the action of one individual partner not only binds the firm legally but makes all other partners personally liable as well, that is, all their personal assets are at risk.

I was a McKinsey partner for 17 years prior to our incorporation. That experience, together with client opportunities I have had to study other true personal service partnerships (accounting and law), has convinced me that working in a partnership is inherently more effective, more productive, and more personally satisfying than working in a typical corporation under command-and-control managing.

Only someone who has been a true partner can appreciate how effectively partners work together, and how close they feel personally. Each must trust the others—not only to be honest, but to carry his or her share of responsibility for defending and developing the firm. Each must support the others and not in any way compete with the others. "One for all, all for one" is more than a slogan. In the early years at McKinsey, there were great risks but also great satisfactions.

So trust, support, personal closeness, the opportunity for profit— along with fear of personal financial loss—combine to create an incentive that typically brings out the very best in the partners (as individuals) and provides them with strong motivation and great personal satisfaction.

Regardless of numbers of shares held, all partners are usually equals, except the head of the firm, who is "first among equals." Any partner can (and should) speak up in criticism, and partners don't hesitate to dissent in the interests of the firm. Thus, partnerships foster teamwork rather than individual stardom.

In the mid-1950s, however, our McKinsey partners decided to incorporate so we could establish a profit-sharing plan under U.S. law, which requires that everyone be included in the plan if the partners are to be included. We delayed incorporation for about two years, however, while we made every effort to instill professional standards, our own firm's standards, and the partnership spirit deeply in our soon-to-be informal "partners" and associates. Our purpose was to carry our partnership responsibilities and spirit over into the new corporate form. We believe we have succeeded quite well. But we find it takes intensive and continuous effort to preserve the real and useful partnership spirit.

Nonetheless, the terms "partner" and "partnership" still carry strongly positive connotations, evoking outstanding human qualities and being virtually synonymous with trust; this is why so many companies use the term "partner" informally. We do in McKinsey. Even though it may not be legally accurate, it can bring out some of the best partnership qualities in people. So the use of informal partnership principles may have a place in the design of leadership companies.

Sam Walton, in his autobiography about building (in his lifetime) Wal-Mart Stores into the largest retailing business in the world, tells how he used partnership principles in his command company.

> As much as we love to talk about all the elements that have gone into Wal-Mart's success—merchandising, distribution, technology, market saturation, real estate strategy—the truth is that none of that is the real secret to our unbelievable prosperity. What has carried this company so far so fast is the relationship that we, the managers, have been able to enjoy with our associates. By "associates" we mean those employees out in the stores and in the distribution centers and on the trucks who generally earn an hourly wage for all their hard work. Our relationship with the associates is a partnership in the truest sense. It's the only reason our company has been able to consistently outperform the competition—and even our own expectations.[4]

When a company decides to convert from commanding to leading, I suggest that it, too, call its employees "associates" and treat them as Sam did. But bear in mind that what counts most is not the terminology, but, as Sam says, that "our relationship with the associates is a partnership in the truest sense." A number of companies call their employees associates, but not many have followed through on the relationship as well as Sam did.

Self-Governing Principles. Just as informal partnership principles and terminology may play a useful role in some leadership companies, so also may self-governing (or self-directing) principles. Hence, I offer some observations on how individual proprietorships and small groups run their organizations, which may suggest special ways to run small groups in large companies—for example, a law department, a research laboratory, an artistic design department. In such situations, self-governing principles may be creative and motivating.

Individual business proprietors must run a small group largely by example and participation in the work themselves. Ordinarily, the more effectively the proprietor works, the greater the success of the business will be. "Work" means not only great exertion and long hours, but smart, creative work and ideas that he or she dreams up. And, believe me, the individual proprietor is dreaming all the time.

The challenge in running small, important groups in large companies is to find ways of developing the same kind of productive and creative effectiveness by creating a special atmosphere that frees up and is attractive to individuals. Usually this can be achieved by leaders who win respect and gain credibility.

Shaping and Monitoring the Corporate Culture

At the time I was writing *The Will to Manage* (1964–66), CEOs of successful companies often referred to "our philosophy." The term seemed to cover the basic beliefs that people in the business were expected to hold and be guided by—informal, unwritten guidelines on how people should perform and conduct themselves. Once such a philosophy crystallizes, it becomes a powerful force indeed, and so I wrote, "When one person tells another, 'That's not the way we do things around here,' the advice had better be heeded."

Since then, however, "philosophy" has become "culture," and I have become a student of culture because of its importance. Much has been written about culture, and the late American anthropologist Alfred L. Kroeber had this to say:

> The degree to which every individual is molded by his culture is enormous. We do not ordinarily recognize the full strength of this shaping process, because it happens to everyone, it happens gradually, . . . and usually there is no obvious alternative open anyway. Hence the molding is taken for granted and is accepted . . .[5]

So it is little wonder that every well-established company has an informal (and powerful) culture, even though it may not be recognized or even discussed. Culture develops from "things that work," from behavior that is or is not acceptable, from examples set by the chief executive, from actions by others that are condoned by the chief executive or other high-level executives. Once these informal guidelines for action have crystallized in people's minds, they become powerful guidelines—and everyone had better heed them.

In addition to guiding decision making and behavior of people without their having to ask for guidance, a company's culture largely controls the environment in which its people spend all their working hours. Therefore, the corporate culture should be one of the leadership company's most important sets of guidelines and motivators, and hence an important responsibility of the chief executive to shape and monitor its development and execution.

No matter how a company is run, it should have a written culture and not let an unwritten culture mold itself. If your company culture is not codified now, I suggest that it be done. And if, at a later date, your company decides to become a leadership company, many features of your present culture can be carried over. Meantime, the codified culture will be very useful in guiding decision making, behavior, and action.

The power of corporate culture is often vividly demonstrated when two companies merge and cultural differences prevent their effective melding. When General Electric acquired brokerage firm Kidder, Peabody, the *Wall Street Journal* reported:

> Just about everything that could go wrong with the Kidder merger has. The cultures have clashed, and GE financial units and Kidder at times have competed with each other when they should have been cooperating. GE and Kidder leaders developed widely disparate views of what Kidder should be. Thus, there was confusion among Kidder executives and the impression among subordinates that the firm was rudderless.[6]

It didn't help when GE selected as the Kidder chief executive an outside GE director who had formerly been president of a tool and die company, prompting one Kidder executive to say, "I was thinking what we need around here is a good tool and die man."[7] Finally, the clashes between the two companies became so dispiriting and unprofitable that GE sold Kidder to another brokerage firm, which has even given up the name.

Therefore, I recommend that every company codify its culture, rather than just letting it grow through the inevitable self-molding process. Indeed, most well-managed companies are already recognizing the value of codifying culture.

One of the cultural pioneers, IBM, codified its culture about thirty years ago in three lectures by then chairman Thomas J. Watson, Jr., entitled "A Business and Its Beliefs." Here is a key excerpt:

> . . . I firmly believe that any organization, in order to survive and achieve success, must have a sound set of beliefs on which it premises all its policies and actions.
>
> Next, I believe that the most important single factor in corporate success is faithful adherence to those beliefs.[8]

Watson's lectures were turned into a book and were used in IBM's executive training courses until recently. These beliefs have become ingrained in IBM people. Now the culture must be changed, and the new chief executive, Lou Gerstner, is finding that this is not easy. In early 1994, a *Wall Street Journal* article observed:

> For more than a year Mr. Gerstner has strained mightily to rescue IBM. He has whacked at costs and has divined a new strategy with a sharper customer focus. But he has been struggling in his toughest and most critical task: forcing changes in an entrenched, patriarchal culture.[9]

The difficulties of effecting changes in culture demonstrate the powerful guidelines that culture provides for running a business, and how—in a leadership company—the culture itself helps leaders lead.

But right here, let me stress a critical point. When a command-and-control company converts to a leadership company, the changes will be so extensive that there must be an altogether new culture statement. It is not enough to make drastic changes in the old one.

Some basic values and principles may carry over, but the two culture statements will have such basically different thrusts that people using leadership will enjoy following the new culture.

I know the power of culture firsthand. In McKinsey we employ most associates directly from graduate schools, and we train them early in our values and guiding principles, which make up our culture. We employ many others who are young but a few years out of graduate school, and a high proportion of them can convert from a business culture to a professional culture. But further along in their prior experience, converting to a profession and adapting to our culture are both difficult; so our success rate with this group is low. Still, our spectacular successes encourage us to continue to take risks with these high-caliber, high-talent, more experienced people who have been advised of the risk they are taking.

But in 1989, McKinsey made a mistake, and I was a party to it. A firm in our field came to us and asked to join. We agreed, departing from our long-term policy of "no mergers." Most of the people who joined were obviously talented and of high caliber, and many of them clearly professionals. In my view, we simply did not try hard enough to help them understand our culture and make them feel at home. Perhaps it would have been impossible. Anyway, most of them left, thus showing the power of culture.

What form should a culture statement take? A Business Roundtable report shows great variety among the hundred companies covered: codes of conduct, creeds, statements of values, statements of ethics, business conduct guidelines, "our guiding management practices," and many other written forms. In short, there is no standard format. IBM took a small book and Johnson & Johnson's "Credo" a single page. (See next page.)

In a speech in December 1983, James E. Burke, then chairman of Johnson & Johnson, said this about the credo:

> I believe in the credo with a passion because I believe in the long run every institution in society has to serve all of its constituencies or it doesn't survive.
>
> What the credo says is that the first thing you have to do is be

Johnson & Johnson

Our Credo

We believe our first responsibility is to the doctors, nurses and patients, to mothers and fathers and all others who use our products and services. In meeting their needs everything we do must be of high quality. We must constantly strive to reduce our costs in order to maintain reasonable prices. Customers' orders must be serviced promptly and accurately. Our suppliers and distributors must have an opportunity to make a fair profit.

We are responsible to our employees, the men and women who work with us throughout the world. Everyone must be considered as an individual. We must respect their dignity and recognize their merit. They must have a sense of security in their jobs. Compensation must be fair and adequate, and working conditions clean, orderly and safe. We must be mindful of ways to help our employees fulfill their family responsibilities. Employees must feel free to make suggestions and complaints. There must be equal opportunity for employment, development and advancement for those qualified. We must provide competent management, and their actions must be just and ethical.

We are responsible to the communities in which we live and work and to the world community as well. We must be good citizens—support good works and charities and bear our fair share of taxes. We must encourage civic improvements and better health and education. We must maintain in good order the property we are privileged to use, protecting the environment and natural resources.

Our final responsibility is to our stockholders. Business must make a sound profit. We must experiment with new ideas. Research must be carried on, innovative programs developed and mistakes paid for. New equipment must be purchased, new facilities provided and new products launched. Reserves must be created to provide for adverse times. When we operate according to these principles, the stockholders should realize a fair return.

totally involved with the people who use your product and services. If you don't, it's a simple fact of life you will die, because someone else will be.

The second thing it says is that the most important raw material you have is the employees. It is their creative energies that do it, after all. Everybody has money and the other things required for success. What's really required is the creative ability of people.

The third thing that it says is if you ignore the communities that you deal with—whether they be the local communities where you have your plants or state or federal communities or just the community of man—your employees and your customers are going to get involved in that process. It is going to redound to your detriment.

Finally, if you do all these things and remind yourself that you are here for the stockholder, you will serve him well.[10]

The Role of Ethics in Corporate Culture. Because of fraud and cheating in major companies, today's corporate community is engaged in an intense discussion of ethics in business. This in turn has brought a new burst of interest in corporate culture. In 1988, the Business Roundtable issued a report called *Corporate Ethics: A Prime Business Asset.* However, the support for ethics as a "prime business asset" is bland and general. The fact is that since the date of the report, readers of the business press can easily recall that companies of stature have been guilty of cheating customers, some of whom have settled for large sums.

So far as I know, however, all the companies involved in the Roundtable report have adhered to high ethical standards. Their example is obviously important in helping to maintain high standards for business in general. For business is critical to the economy, and high ethical standards are critical to business. That obvious statement deserves support by everyone.

Ethical Business Principles Build Trust—and Profits. That business ethics can be profitable has been documented by James E. Burke, former chairman of Johnson & Johnson. In connection with the Advertising Council's Award for Public Service that Jim received, he and his staff studied 26 companies that had written sets of socially responsible principles and determined their financial results over 30 years. Jim says:

I believe strongly in the moral imperative of companies serving the public in the broadest possible sense. That's what intrigued me about doing this study. The results were eye-opening, though all along I suspected how it would come out. What we found was that those companies with a written commitment to be socially responsible recorded an average 10.7 percent growth in profits compounded over 30 years. This was 1.34 times better than the growth of the gross national product over the same period.

The study included examples of how investments in these companies would have done over the 30-year period, and the results were striking.

If any one of you had invested $30,000 in a composite of the Dow Jones 30 years ago, it would be worth $134,000 today. If you had invested the same $30,000—$2,000 in each of the companies remaining in the survey—your $30,000 would be worth over $1,000,000—*$1,021,861* to be exact! (If the Dow had grown at the same rate as these companies, it would be over 9,000—9,399 to be exact.)[11]

Sir Adrian Cadbury, chairman of Cadbury Schweppes PLC, in a prize-winning article in the *Harvard Business Review*, asserts that openness and ethics go together and that actions are unethical if they will not stand public scrutiny. Openness in arriving at decisions reflects the same logic. It gives people with an interest in a particular decision the chance to make their views known. Also, openness is the best way to disarm outside suspicion of a company's motives and actions.[12]

When Harvey Golub, now chairman of American Express, was head of the IDS Financial Services division, he wrote an article titled "Ethics: Sure, it's easy to say that you're pure, but just try teaching your employees right from wrong":

At IDS Financial Services, we have rigorous ethical standards that govern everything we do. And we're absolutely serious about living up to them. There is very little *gray* area: Something is either right—or wrong. And because our values are clear, we believe it's easier for our people, from the bottom to the top, to make the right decisions about how this company should operate.[13]

A culture statement should clearly state that everyone in the company is expected to tell the truth inside and outside the company on all occasions—not only because the truth is important in itself, but because the best way to establish trust is to be consistently truthful. And trust throughout a leadership company creates a supportive atmosphere for leaders and their constituents.

Establishing a Motivating Corporate Purpose

A motivating corporate purpose (or mission) is a vital stepping stone to running a business with a network of leaders. It should, if possible, motivate everyone in the company. Thus, it will help attract people with leadership capabilities, and may help to attract outstanding people in choosing careers.

People with the capacity to lead want to do something *worthwhile;* and that is the type of person a leadership company should try to attract at all levels. So a motivating purpose should be included in the company's culture statement.

In recent years, however, the fashionable corporate purpose has been to increase shareholder wealth. I totally disagree. Increasing shareholder wealth does not do justice to business as an institution. Certainly there is nothing in the shareholder-wealth purpose that suggests teamwork; in fact, just the reverse is true.

Consider what associates who have risky or boring jobs on the production line might think to themselves or say to each other: "Why should I go through this stuff all day long for those lousy rich shareholders?" (Only the language would probably be earthier.)

Consider even the attitudes of people with more attractive jobs. Won't they also question why they should work as hard as they do—or put up with the boredom they do—for the primary benefit of shareholders?

Of course, by making all associates shareholders, the sharp negative edge of shareholder-wealth purpose can be dulled. Even then, however, the obvious disparity in numbers of shares owned by different associates and executives means that shareholder wealth will provide little motivation for everyone to work together as a team. And, of course, shareholders are not the only constituency to which a corporation is responsible.

Increasing shareholder wealth requires a short-term focus on raising share prices. (One CEO asked his secretary to give him company share prices every day at 11:00 A.M. and 2:00 P.M.) And short-term thinking will not ordinarily produce the strongest competitiveness or largest long-term profits.

I believe that the best corporate purpose is to achieve customer satisfaction; this is a good motivator for people to work together to improve the company's share of market, competitiveness, and profitability. In fact, there is a worldwide trend to gain competitiveness by focusing on serving customers with better-quality products and better-quality services at competitive prices: a concept expressed long ago by Peter Drucker, Ted Levitt, and a few other farsighted thinkers and writers on managing.

In McKinsey I have always advocated the concept that "earnings are a by-product of serving clients well." If our services bring real value to our clients, our earnings will come as a by-product. That is true in a profession, and I believe the same concept applies in a business, as indeed, Jim Burke confirmed earlier.

Joyce C. Hall, founder of Hallmark Cards, Inc., in his autobiography, *When You Care Enough*, wrote:

> If a man goes into business only with the idea of making a lot of money, chances are he won't. But if he puts service and quality first, the money will take care of itself. Producing a first-class product that is a real need is a much stronger motivation for success than getting rich."[14]

From a different national culture, Konosuke Matsushita, founder and Chairman Emeritus of Matsushita Electric and founder of the leadership chair in his name at Harvard Business School, expressed the same general conclusion:

> . . . If you grant that a business exists because it is necessary to society—because it responds to people's needs—the basic rule of

management is self-evident: learn what the people want and respond accordingly. Of course, one must be conscientious in his efforts to serve the people and do his best to satisfy them. I have made this my basic principle since I founded Matsushita Electric more than sixty years ago.[15]

Pursuing that mission, Matsushita Electric has become the 17th largest company in the Fortune Global 500, with 1994 sales of $69.9 billion and profits of $911 million.

The 1995 annual report of Merck & Co., Inc., is titled "Building Our Business by Serving Society."

Sam Walton states Wal-Mart's mission this way:

. . . We exist to provide value to our customers, which means that in addition to quality and service, we have to save them money. Every time Wal-Mart spends one dollar foolishly, it comes right out of our customers' pockets. Every time we save them a dollar, that puts us one more step ahead of the competition—which is where we always plan to be.[16]

That statement is clear, precise, and motivating. It even explains the company's strategy.

Leaders throughout a leadership company can confidently use the mission statement to motivate other leaders and associates to work together effectively, efficiently, harmoniously, and even enthusiastically.

Even when you heartily endorse your company's purpose, it isn't always easy to create a mission statement that does not sound platitudinous to some. Don't worry about it. By giving deep thought to the purpose and to the most motivating way of stating it for your people, you and the other company leaders can bring handsome rewards to the business. For, in a leadership company, creating the statement of purpose is a task for all leaders, not just the top management.

Developing a Corporate Vision

It is even more difficult to develop a corporate vision: an imaginative, inspirational "picture" that energizes people to focus on corporate purpose.

After reorganizing the company to include only service businesses, Harvey Golub, chairman of American Express, decided on this vision statement: "to become the world's most respected service brand."[17]

Johnson & Johnson—a family of some 165 health-care companies—has a useful vision: "We all want to live longer and healthier lives."[18] That is clearly a motivational thought for everyone in the company to think about on the way to work.

On the other hand, to say that "we want to be number one or number two in any industry in which we operate" is hardly a vision statement. That is more a measure than a motivator, or a form of control for a command-and-control company, not a motivating vision for a leadership company.

Many companies keep struggling for a motivating vision. They can't all be as lucky as J&J. Some may take the form of an advertising slogan. IBM has recently begun using this slogan: "Solutions for a small planet." General Electric: "We bring good things to life." Delta Airlines: "You'll love the way we fly." United Parcel Service: "Moving at the speed of business."

SIX

Leadership Design:
The Roles of Teams

WHEN I FIRST began thinking about leadership as a "total" way to run a business, the use of teams in American business was gathering momentum. About the same time, two McKinsey colleagues, Jon R. Katzenbach and Douglas K. Smith, were writing a book called *The Wisdom of Teams* (Harvard Business School Press, 1993; hereafter abbreviated *Wisdom*) which went on to become a best-selling business book.

McKinsey has always used teams to serve our clients. But as I learned more about business teams, it became evident that they could be built into leadership teams that could carry leadership throughout the business. And along with leadership teams can go individual leaders to make up part of the network. Thus, the company would not be dependent on the chief executive alone for leadership. But more important, leaders and leadership teams scattered strategically throughout the company will spread the power of leadership, and hence should vastly improve company performance.

Given our long experience with teams, it was natural that we use them to run the firm itself. Each individual office has a leader who runs the office as a leadership team of partners. And there are leadership teams within each office and within the firm overall to carry on various activities. The leaders of these teams are first among equals. I mention this merely to show that I draw on experience with both operating and leadership teams.

Operating Teams

Wisdom defines a "real" team as a small group of people (typically fewer than 20) with complementary skills committed to a common purpose, performance goals, and an approach for which they hold themselves mutually accountable. (Let's call that an "operating team" to distinguish it from a "leadership team," which we will take up next.)

Giving us a deeper understanding of "real" operating teams, an article based on *Wisdom* says:

> Savvy managers have always known that real teams—not just groups of people with a label attached—will invariably outperform the same set of individuals operating in a non-team mode, particularly where multiple skills, experiences, and judgments determine performance. Being more flexible than larger organizational groupings, they can be more quickly and effectively assembled, deployed, refocused, and disbanded. And being more firmly and mutually committed to tangible performance results, they can more readily leverage their combined skills to achieve objectives beyond the reach of less tightly-bound collections of individuals.[1]

None of this is new. Ancient generals understood the wisdom of teams no less than do modern corporate leaders. What makes that wisdom of such importance now—and so worth the urgent attention of top management—is not novelty but the proven link between teams, individual behavioral change, and high performance.

More and more we are finding that behavioral change occurs more readily when people work in teams than when they work alone. Their collective commitment and focus on performance motivates team members to try to alter the way they do things, that is, they consciously and subconsciously try to change their behavior. In teams, learning also occurs more readily—just as people working together to institutionalize leadership in a company will learn to lead better and faster than they would as individuals working alone.

Teams are becoming so common that to get them started in a company does not call for a broadside announcement. Indeed, it may be better to start them in two or three plants or departments—or in a well-known problem area—and let their success create a demand for more teams.

To get operating teams off to a good start, however, requires some guidance. One approach is to select an appropriate executive who in turn appoints a team monitor charged with making a quick study of teams to learn the requirements for team success. Because the team must be self-directing, the monitor's role will be to answer questions and give knowledgeable guidance to team members, but not tell them what to do.

Step 2 is for the executive and the team monitor to lay out the broad purpose of the team and a broad performance goal, that is, to develop a sort of "charter."

Step 3 is to select prospective team members. These should include one or two people with the appropriate technical or functional skills, and one or two people with skills or gifts in problem solving, risk taking, objectivity, active listening, and recognizing the achievements and interests of others.

Next, the executive calls the team members together, and with the help of the team monitor, describes the kind of work that is currently being done by operating teams across the country, and the kinds of success these teams have achieved.

Together, the executive and the team monitor explain the self-managing character of effective teams, and point out that, as team members, they will select their own leaders and be free to change leaders to fit new circumstances as they develop.

The executive and the team monitor then describe what they think the broad purpose or "team charter" should be and why. But because they know it is essential that team members buy into the charter, they invite them to discuss it, refine it, challenge it, and even develop and recommend a better charter. Once a broad purpose is agreed on, the team members must then set performance goals tied to that purpose.

Next, the executive and the team monitor stress the need for team members to commit themselves to the collective achievement of these goals and to recognition that responsibility for achieving the goals rests with the team as a whole, not with the leader or with any individual member.

Finally, they offer a few guidelines for team behavior such as striving for objectivity in discussing problem areas, recognizing one another's interests and achievements, and learning to trust one another, and not compete with one another.

After this orientation, the team should take off on its own, with no interference or control by anyone, and with only monitoring and mentoring from the team monitor. This approach should encourage people to get involved and make their many capabilities available through teams. In time, team successes will demonstrate their value and galvanize their use throughout the company.

Regardless of the way you run your business now or expect to run it in the future, if your company does not already have operating teams, I suggest that you set some up. Many might be temporary because their purpose will be to solve specific problems. But whether they are temporary or long-term to permanent, these teams can be highly effective performance units. Moreover, they provide good training for leaders of leadership teams should your company ever decide to move toward running the business through a network of leaders. (See also Worthwhile Reading.)

Leadership Teams

Leadership teams are a distinguishing characteristic of a leadership company. Although similar in many ways to an operating team, leadership teams do have major differences.

First, unlike the operating team, leadership teams do not select their own leaders. But the leader of these teams must be a true leader, that is, he or she must be able to gain the trust of the other team members and thereby turn them into constituents. The mutual trust between leader and constituents encourages open communication; constituents feel free to express their ideas and views, and disagree with each other, including the leader. Thus, there is no hierarchy within the leadership team—no "superiors," no "subordinates." All members are equals, except that the leader is "first among equals."*

---

* This important term—*primus inter pares,* or "first among equals"—gives the leader special authority to resolve differences among equals and to have special higher authority over the others that the leader will exercise infrequently.

Each leader (of a leadership team) must have or must learn most of these additional qualities or attributes: unassuming behavior, fairness, willingness to listen, an open mind, sensitivity to people and situations, flexibility and adaptability, initiative, good judgment, broad-mindedness, and sense of urgency—all as discussed in Chapter 3. You will observe that these attributes are similar to those of the CEO, but they need not be learned in the same depth, and so should be less difficult to learn. Moreover, these attributes will improve with experience.

Later, these leaders will learn to make timely decisions and develop the capacity to motivate, both of which will require much more experience. And, of course, each degree of learning will vary from person to person and attribute to attribute.

You should note that leaders of these teams are not expected to have the capacity to develop company goals or visions. Those targets are provided by the CEO and other top leaders, and communicated to these leaders who, in turn, communicate them to their constituents. However, these team leaders should feel free to contribute (if they can) to shaping company goals and visions as part of their contributions to strategy (as discussed in the next chapter).

Further, each of these leaders has the same responsibilities to his or her constituents that the chief executive has to constituents, except that these leaders can't be expected to discharge their responsibilities as well as the CEO. As discussed in Chapter 5, they must:

- Treat constituents with respect.

- Build constituents' self-confidence and self-esteem, and make them feel good about themselves.

- Based on information transmitted by the coordinators, make them feel they have a real stake in the company's present performance and future success. (See Chapter 8.)

- Help all constituents develop as individuals.

All these points are discussed in Chapters 3 and 4.

Leadership teams are positioned to become effective vehicles for deploying leadership strategically to different parts of the business, along with individual leaders who do not lead teams. These assignments would be made on the basis of the degree of leadership required for different activities and the degrees of leadership effectiveness learned by different individuals.

Thus, the benefits of leadership permeate the leadership company, together with initiative, new ideas, and good judgment developed through the resolution of differences of opinion within teams.

Leadership teams are typically more permanent than operating teams but can easily be changed with conditions. And leaders and their constituents can be changed individually. Thus, leadership teams make for flexibility; they don't experience the trauma of change that comes with "reorganization" in a command company; that term delineates new lines of authority and changes in responsibility among individual superiors and subordinates that cause resistance to change. In fact, "organization structure," which defines authority and responsibility, will be extinct in a leadership company. Leadership teams and individual leaders are a part of the leadership company design that will be discussed in the next chapter.

The Chairman's Team

Let us now take up a unique leadership team, the team at the top. Although designed for a leadership company, it can also improve managing in a command-and-control company.

The chairman's team is made up of the chief executive and one or two carefully chosen senior executives who would be co-equals with the chief executive. There would be no hierarchy; all three (or two) would take an on-the-job crash course in leadership so they can work together as equals. Like true partners, they would trust each other. Each could speak for the others. Each could disagree with the others, including the chairman. And the chairman (as first among equals) would resolve differences.

Indeed, this may be the only way the board of a company with a single all-powerful chief executive can avoid putting at risk the wealth of the corporation and the well-being of employees (and their families).

As we have seen, when a command-and-control company falters seriously, the board replaces the chief executive with someone from outside the company or advances someone from within. The boards of IBM, Westinghouse, and Kodak went outside; the GM and Digital Equipment boards advanced the new CEO from within. In each of these cases, however, the new chief executive also became a single, all-powerful individual. And whatever leading each does, he does from the top.

These new CEOs have substantially full authority to overrule anyone else and authority to change the hierarchy below. Indeed, these companies are simply changing one all-powerful CEO for another. Those new to the company were selected on the basis of their records, performance, interviews, and other careful checking. There is no way that these new CEOs from the outside could have acquired a real understanding of the company's problems or people before accepting the job.

How long, then, should the board wait for profit improvement before replacing the new chief? (GM's board waited about two years before advancing another person from inside.) How much time should the new CEOs of other companies be given, and for what degree of company profit improvement?

As I've said, I believe that the limitations of command-and-control managing are largely to blame for corporate faltering. But it is difficult to separate these limitations from the all-powerful CEO's personal qualities and abilities. Time marches on inexorably, a day at a time. Only the CEO or the board can say, "Today's the day for crisis action." And only the board can say, "The time has come to change the CEO."

If the company converts from commanding to a leadership company, the risks of having a single CEO will be significantly fewer: The chief executive as a leader would listen, and his or her constituents would speak up and disagree if necessary.

However, with only one leader at the top, the company is also vulnerable to that person's physical weaknesses and limitations—a real risk. Tenneco, in 1991 a faltering Fortune 500 company, brought in an outstanding person as the new chief executive. He died of cancer two years later despite his valiant efforts following an operation.

In July 1994, Michael Eisner, chairman of Walt Disney Company, had emergency quadruple bypass heart surgery that the company announced would keep him from work for several weeks. Three months earlier, the company's president had died in a helicopter accident.[2]

The Disney/ABC merger in August 1995 put more pressure on Eisner. In fact he seemed to acknowledge the need for more help at the top: The week following the merger he hired his close friend, Michael Ovitz, the head of Creative Artists Agency, to be his "No. 2 man." "I am the chairman," he told the *New York Times*. "I need a partner. We will understand each other's moves. The company is big and growing, and Michael joins a team that is very strong."[3] But they are not co-leaders: Eisner is the boss. (However, Ovitz left Disney after only 18 months.[4])

Clearly, the time for the board to consider establishing a chairman's team is when the company is performing well, and I strongly advocate that it be considered. In addition to reducing a real risk, it's a way of testing the viability of a leadership team at the top while command-and-control managing continues. In other words, a command-and-control company can experiment with such a team without committing itself to becoming a leadership company. The sophisticated reader will say, "What's new about a chairman's team?" My answer is that the chairman's team I have described is a leadership team and that *would* be new.

Today teams at the top with such names as "Chairman's Office" and "Office of the CEO" are fairly common in large corporations, but these are *not* leadership teams.

Take this real example of a team at the top that is not a leadership team: One of the country's largest corporations had a chairman's office that included three vice chairmen who had no specific responsibilities except to help the chairman manage the business. When I asked one of these vice chairmen whether he had told the chairman about a serious problem facing the company, he replied, "Do you think I'd tell him about that when I'm bucking for his job?" So this office was a "group," not a team, and within the group there was hierarchy. The vice chairman would not level with the chairman, because the chairman was really his boss. (And, believe me, he *was* his boss.)

In organizing the chairman's team, the chairman would, of course, consult with the board and with its approval invite one or two senior executives to join the team. Then, together, they would learn to become leaders, thus making it a leadership team of co-equals with the chairman as first among equals.

The chairman might (or might not) tell the others that he or she was considering the possibility of becoming a leadership company, and that, sometime in the future, the chairman's team would decide whether to recommend this major change to the board.

By learning to become leaders together, the team members would accelerate the learning process, would gain hands-on experience in learning the advantages of leading instead of relying on authority to get things done, and would detect any personal difficulties they and perhaps others might have in learning to lead. Altogether, they would acquire a sounder basis for judging whether to convert to a leadership company.

I can cite two teams of this kind that have worked well for two large companies, although neither has become a leadership company.

The Royal Dutch/Shell Group. McKinsey's first study for the Royal Dutch/Shell Group was of the Group's largest operating company in Venezuela in 1956. The Group was then headed by a team composed of the late John Loudon, chairman, and six managing directors, all seven of whom were co-equals. John thought of himself as "primus inter pares"—first among equals—and so did everyone else.

There was no hierarchy within this Shell team; all were involved collectively in running the worldwide corporation. There were no assigned individual responsibilities, but "spheres of interest" were assigned to each managing director without his becoming responsible for decisions in his sphere. Each individual kept the others informed for the team's overall decision making.

John Loudon, as a true international leader, got most things done by example and the rest by persuasion and suggestion. He was so trusted and respected, so willing to listen and so open-minded, and his judgment so highly regarded, that his six co-leaders seemed to find him a positive pleasure to work with.

The McKinsey team that served Shell on that occasion was similarly organized. I was managing director of McKinsey at the time and also served as head of our Shell team. Hugh Parker, a seasoned consultant, was leader when I was not there; and Lee Walton, an outstanding associate but of only a couple of years' tenure, was the third "permanent" member of the team. Hugh and Lee moved to Caracas, and the three of us led the other consultants who came and went for specialized work. I spent about three weeks at a time in Caracas.

Our team was a true leadership team, with no hierarchy within the team, no matter how many other team members attended each decision-making meeting in Caracas. Anyone could speak up; anyone could disagree with anyone else. We had many differences of opinion on issues of major importance. I recall particularly that Lee Walton put forward many important recommendations that were thrashed out, only a few of which did I have to decide as "first among equals." So did Hugh, but that was expected. For us, there was nothing unusual in this way of working, but I can recall clearly that many associates were significant contributors to the important recommendations on which Shell acted.

Not long after the Shell study, Hugh Parker became leader of our London office, and many years later Lee was elected managing director of McKinsey.

Goldman, Sachs. Goldman, Sachs has had three generations of co-chairmen at the top; and teams and teamwork have been integral to its success for many years. From 1976 to 1984, John Weinberg and John Whitehead served as co-chairmen. And they were followed by two other teams of co-chairmen.

At a McKinsey partners' conference on teamwork in 1994, the partners viewed videotaped interviews with a number of our client chief executives. Among them was John Whitehead, whose observations on chairmen's teams are a must-read for any CEO who is considering a team at the top. This is why, with his permission, you'll find the full transcript in Appendix A.

Advantages of a Chairman's Team: A Summary

A leadership team at the top consists of two or three co-leaders who become close personal partners working together to achieve the goal of the business and setting a noble example for other companies to follow.

1. As companies grow in size, become more complex, and expand geographically, no single chief executive can discharge his or her responsibilities effectively. To cope with growth, command companies add hierarchy, thus making managing even more cumbersome.

   With a chairman's team, however, another member of the chairman's team can act for the chairman, or members can act collectively. Leadership responsibilities can be divided into "spheres of interest" among the members; and the spheres can be rotated from time to time.

2. The team of two or three can keep a closer watch on competitive forces than a single chief. The team also has a better chance of detecting opportunities for moving the company ahead or for coping with threats from direct or indirect competition.

3. On important issues, such as mergers, acquisitions, or selling parts of the business, two or three co-leaders can act as one. These are issues (such as, can the two different corporate cultures be joined successfully?) where the chairman must either be richly endowed with intuition or have keen perceptions if he or she is to make a sound decision. And here is where the other members of the team (of equals) can meld their intuitions and perceptions with the chairman's.

4. In the privacy of their discussions, other members of the team are free to disagree with the chairman and sharply criticize one another. This removes much of the hidden risk of having a single chief executive whom others hold in awe.

5. In a chairman's team, any member can bring up major initiatives the others may have overlooked.

6. A leadership team is a real team; and real teams facilitate the learning and behavioral development of their members. Even members of the chairman's team accelerate one another's learning of leadership on the job.

7. The chairman's team protects the company from a single executive's potential health problems.

SEVEN

Custom-Designing the Network

CEOs ARE no longer only voicing their dissatisfaction with command-and-control managing, but calling for active experimentation with new ways of running companies. For example, in an excellent article in *Chief Executive*, Irvine 0. Hockaday, president and CEO of Hallmark Cards, a privately owned $4 billion publisher of greeting cards, describes what he believes must be done:

> . . . I believe we as CEOs must move our companies away from the hierarchical, command-and-control management style that has long characterized American business and toward a model based on teamwork, communication, flexibility, and employee empowerment. . . . such a transformation will enhance not only our ability as businesses to achieve and sustain high performance, but also the competitive position and social well-being of the U.S. . . .[1]

As Mr. Hockaday says, the movement away from command managing is "toward a *model* based on teamwork, communication, flexibility, and employee empowerment. . . ." Leadership does that, I believe. But after an extensive search for a company that has some form of *institutionalized* leadership below the level of chief executive, I have found none. So I have no model that other companies might emulate.

Approach to Leadership Company Development

As I said at the outset of this book, the best I can offer is a cockshy, something to shoot at. Even that cannot be very precise for a hypothetical company. But having thought for a number of years about running a business with a network of leaders, I can describe what I hope are some useful possibilities for reader consideration.

Improving Top-Management Performance. If you are chief executive of a command company and are developing the will to lead, I believe you will manage the company substantially and noticeably better by taking the following leadership steps now:

1. Lay a foundation for leading: Practice trustworthiness; be unassuming; listen with an open and acquiring mind; be fair and considerate with people; and be flexible and willing to change. I believe you will find that many of these attributes are already part of your behavior and need only further recognition and emphasis.

2. Help your direct reports develop self-confidence and self-esteem and feel good about themselves. This, in itself, will set you apart as a leader and motivate others toward leading.

As you improve your leading in these ways, I believe you will observe how positively your constituents (your former subordinates) will respond, especially when you listen to them and help them develop self-confidence and self-esteem. Also, if you, the chief executive, experiment with learning leadership on the job, you will gain leadership-learning experience yourself. Thus, the whole top-management group will be strengthened.

Establishing Real Operating Teams. This is *not* an experimental step. Regardless of the way the business is run now, operating teams (whether permanent or temporary) can be highly effective performance units. You may have such teams already. What is relevant here is that these teams will also provide good training for people to become leaders of leadership teams.

Approach to Conversion

If, instead, you decide to experiment now with becoming a leadership company, here are three initial guidelines:

Become a role model. Keep polishing your leadership through action. Set a sparkling example. Get people excited about the company's conversion to leadership, and as excited about their performance as you are about your own.

Establish a leadership development team. This team would (initially) be a single person (from within the company) who would help the CEO with all phases of research, experimentation, planning, and action. As the conversion expands, additional people would be added to the team. The head of the team should be selected for leadership potential and should actively pursue the goal of becoming a leader.

Don't rush conversion. There is no need for speed—no need for an overall master plan. Rather, conversion should be done a step at a time, providing opportunities for creativity and experimentation. And during this period the company can be run partly through authority and partly through leading. If replacing leading becomes necessary, the very nature of authority will make it easy to return to the former command way of running the company; that possibility removes much of the risk of starting on conversion.

Scoping the Learning. Replacing bosses with leaders will present such an exciting prospect that I believe people will *want* to make the change. When the decision to convert to a leadership company has been made, however, there will be many questions, such as How will I "get ahead" and What about my compensation? The chief executive must reassure the new leaders and their constituents that such related policies will also be made, and *with their participation.*

Those other than the CEO will undoubtedly have a harder time learning to become leaders, but the leading they must learn will also be less difficult. All leaders, of course, will be responsible for training their constituents. They, in turn, must learn that they are responsible for expressing their views candidly to leaders; that they can differ and disagree with anyone, even the chief executive; and that they must always strive for the best possible decisions and actions. Constituents will have far greater knowledge to impart than they ever had in a hierarchy; and leaders will be able to leverage this knowledge to even greater advantage in making decisions and taking action.

But unless people overcome their awe of their former bosses, including the chief executive, some of leadership's great value to a business will be lost.

Setting Up a Framework for the Design. At the outset, the chief executive and the board should select two or three senior executives (reporting to the CEO) to serve as coordinators. These coordinators should learn to become leaders as rapidly as possible.

Individual leaders, leadership teams, and working groups should be assigned to coordinators in whatever way makes sense for that company. Thus, all individual leaders and leadership teams that make up the network will be assigned to one of the two or three coordinators.

The development team would assist in developing the design, in selecting individuals as candidates for leaders, and in positioning them in key areas. This team would also have responsibility for helping leaders and constituents learn on the job.

The guide to network designing would start with the company's present organization chart and a list of all departments and positions. All present command-and-control activities would need to be assigned to individual leaders, leadership teams, or working groups with a leader. Some present activities might be dropped, and others might be added. Indeed, some leadership teams could be designed around individuals who have specialized knowledge and who are clearly leader candidates. And, of course, people with specialized knowledge would be placed in relevant teams.

This would be the occasion for a clean-sheet-of-paper redesign of the whole business, with everyone assigned to becoming an individual leader, a team leader, a constituent of some leader, or a member of a working group headed by a leader. Assignments would include plant workers and other operating personnel, even though the teams or groups may be large ones.

Obviously, this complex task of designing will take time. Even more time will be required to develop individual leaders and leaders of teams, and to train constituents. Hence, during this transition period, when the company is run in a hybrid manner, there would be a gradual emergence from commanding to leading—all under the leadership of the chief executive and the coordinating leaders, with the help of the development team. Moreover, individual leaders throughout the company would participate as well.

Thus, all individual leaders and leadership teams would be stationed strategically throughout the company and, at the appropriate time, their coordinators would select individuals to become leader candidates.

Again, conversion to a leadership company really requires making the company over; this is an advantage because it encourages creativity and experimentation. Indeed, I believe that ingenuity in leadership design will provide competitive advantages and more enjoyable working conditions.

There will be no need for an organization chart. Such a chart shows positions, responsibilities, and lines of authority, who reports to whom: in other words, a "visual" for hierarchy. In a leadership company, coordination is provided through relationships—who leads whom. So after all present command-and-control activities and people have been assigned, there might be a design diagram showing these "coordinating relationships."

The opportunity to shift relationships among individual leaders and leadership teams, and to change the makeup of teams, provides one of the great advantages of a leadership company—flexibility. With hierarchy gone, resistance of individuals to change should decline and could even disappear. Again, this may mean that during the transition period, the company would be run as a hybrid of authority and leading.

But before describing types of teams, let's discuss how a network of leadership teams might work to enable people to work together more effectively, efficiently, and harmoniously. Let's start with an example—a single leadership marketing team made up of a team leader and, say, five constituents. The team is located close to the scene of the action, so constituents can gather facts, develop opinions, and get ideas.

At a meeting of the leadership team called to discuss an idea for a new product, the leader opened in this way.

"The company is experimenting with the possibility of converting to a leadership company. This is the first meeting of our team, and I want to urge each of you to speak your minds. You have received a memo from me about a possible new product, and today we'll take a first cut at it.

"But first, I'd like to talk about how a leadership team works. We are going to eliminate hierarchy, which means that we will all become peers. I will not be your boss. We can all disagree with one another, and each of you can disagree with me. If I can't persuade you, and we can't reach agreement, I will resolve the issues because, as leader, I'm what they call 'first among equals.' But I won't take that action unless it's necessary. This is the beginning of a new world. I hope you'll find it a better world for our company's performance and for each of you individually. It's my job to persuade you that the leadership way is the best way to work together.

"Here are two of my most important responsibilities:

- "First, to develop *your* self-confidence so you will feel free to speak up, take initiatives whenever you wish, get ideas whenever you can, and tell the rest of us about them.

- "Next, to think about the company as a whole and to discuss it that way—not to talk just about marketing, but about our competitive position and how we make profits. We want you to develop ideas about other parts of the business—manufacturing, for example. We want you to feel you are a real part of the company.

"I'm new at my job, and I hope you will all help me learn. I'm going to listen with an open mind; if I don't, jog me about it.

"Before we begin talking about our possible new product, let's talk about these new ways of operating. And let's remember that we must all develop trust in each other."

The team discussed the new leadership program, liked the idea, and then took up the new product. It concluded that the idea was worth pursuing and decided to gather more facts.

When the team met two weeks later, opinions were mixed about the marketability of the product; everyone agreed that still more facts were needed, including manufacturing costs. So a manufacturing leadership team was brought in.

Representatives of the manufacturing team reached agreement

on the estimated costs of the new product. The marketing team met again to consider reducing estimated manufacturing costs and to discuss additional facts. Thereafter, the two teams decided that the new product was not worth pursuing further, and the idea was dropped.

Had the marketing team developed enthusiasm for the new product, the team's coordinator might have asked for a full meeting of the manufacturing team to get more precise costs. And had the coordinator for the manufacturing team been enthusiastic, he and the coordinator for the marketing team might have met. Then, had the new product required a major investment, they might have taken the decision to the chief financial officer and perhaps to the chief executive.

Leadership teams in a business have no hierarchy, so all members of the team, including the leader, are equals. But if there are differences of opinion within the team, the leader, who is first among equals, should resolve issues.

At McKinsey such leadership teams already work well. The partner, who heads a team, and the associates, who are members of the team, are all equals. If there are differences of opinion, the leader resolves the issues. With experience, I believe such teams would work well in businesses, including those in which multiple teams would work together.

Now let us consider some examples of cockshies a particular company might adopt in developing the design for a leadership company. Logically we would start with strategy. However, I believe that the discussion of strategy will be clearer after we describe some of the leadership teams most companies would establish to replace present departments, plus some new ones.

Cockshies for the Design

I will try to be as specific as possible in describing leadership team examples that might be common among companies. Let me emphasize, however, that the cockshies I offer are not recommendations. I have thought seriously about them, of course, but any company can probably design something more effective for its particular requirements.

And there is no fixed pattern for the way that leaders are assigned or how leaders and leadership teams are strategically stationed. With no company to emulate, the designers must use imagination and engage in experimentation to determine how teams shall be made up and stationed.

Operational Leadership Teams	Advisory Leadership Teams
Finance	Technology Alert
Marketing	Computer Alert
Manufacturing	"Hustle"
Research and Development	Environment
Supplier	Legal
	Strategy

Operational Leadership Teams

Finance Team. Finance is such an important activity for every company that this may provide patterns for other leadership teams. The leader of the finance team is the chief financial officer (CFO), who should be a respected financial authority within the company (and perhaps outside). He or she would be a planner and coordinator of all finance teams: treasurer (banking), controller (accounting), cash flow planning, financing, and so on.

The CFO should be responsible (together with the subfinance teams) for ensuring that the company has adequate cash, a strong balance sheet, and a sound debt-equity ratio—all of which will permit the company to make investments and take risks.

These finance leadership teams should not be simply a conversion of the present setup; indeed, under the leadership of the CFO, this is the opportune time to redesign the whole finance activity. For example, the budgeting function, in the control sense, would not be needed; but the budget executive might take over cash flow planning and impose whatever controls for honesty and integrity may be required in the particular company.

Thus the CFO and the development team would decide on the number and purpose of leadership teams that the specific company requires. Then the leader of each finance leadership team would have meetings with his or her constituents similar to the meeting with the marketing team. Again, these meetings would explain the nature of leadership within each team: how hierarchy is eliminated, how constituents discuss issues with one another and reach conclusions, and how constituents discuss issues with the leader and reach conclusions. Each team would agree to strive for a climate of mutual trust that invites open discussion and the thrashing out of differences of opinion that stimulates creative thinking.

The leader of each finance leadership team would be a constituent of the CFO, who would coordinate them. If the issues involve more than two teams, the CFO would resolve differences of opinion.

Thus the finance activity would be a body of leaders and leadership teams working together to serve the entire enterprise, receiving suggestions and criticisms from other parts of the business, developing and helping others to develop sound financial sense as part of learning to be entrepreneurs.

Some companies will need even stronger controls than some command companies typically have: companies in which individuals (for example, traders) have authority over money or other valuable assets, so that an individual's poor judgment, greed, or dishonesty might put major assets at risk. Perhaps the most lurid recent example is the 28-year-old trader who took such risks that he brought down the legendary Baring Brothers in England.

The CFO, working with the leaders of individual finance teams, would formulate major policies and coordinate finance with other activities. Teams would need to be retitled, but to avoid confusing outsiders, the familiar titles should be preserved, such as "treasurer" and "controller." (However, it might be advisable to change "controller" to its former title: "comptroller"; in the past there was a drive among comptrollers to get the title "controller" so as to indicate their *authority* to "control.")

Finance teams, however, should have a new activity: to provide all leaders and leadership teams throughout the company with financial (and other) information they can use to make informed decisions in moving ahead entrepreneurially on their own. For example, finance teams should provide profit-and-loss information for operations and the cost of capital for operations involved. The CFO should decide which teams should provide what information, some of which should come from other parts of the business. However, information provided for entrepreneurial decision making is not for "control" purposes, as it would be in a hierarchical company.

Finance teams would have a major part in developing the profit-sharing and stock ownership plans, which I recommend be established for all leadership companies. And stock options should be considered. However, the initial, basic planning should be done by a broad-based, temporary operating team under the overall leadership of one of the senior coordinators, with the CFO as a member.

People who are used to working with budgets will have little trouble with operating information. But leaders will have to learn to make informed recommendations on the use of capital. How much capital will a plant or other fixed asset take? How long will the capital be tied up? What will the operating cost be? If all leaders understand such information, they will be more entrepreneurial, a skill which all leaders should try to develop.

Marketing Teams. These teams might follow the finance cockshy with an individual chief marketing officer (CMO) leading a number of leadership marketing teams designed to fit the particular business, such as product development, sales promotion, advertising, and so on. This would be the occasion to consider whether to redesign marketing activities. Policies (such as distribution) can be established jointly by the marketing leaders.

Pricing policy can be established in the same way, but other leaders should also participate. The opportunities in a leadership company for increased profit through skillful pricing are so great that this opportunity should not be overlooked.

Customer-sensing team. A leadership company, with its open-minded leaders scattered strategically throughout the company, provides opportunities to introduce major new ideas. To help formulate and carry out company strategy, every leader should have a sense of the market and the company's customers. The customer-sensing team has responsibility for gathering that information and communicating it to company leaders. Any additional time that leaders spend with customers in the field will make the company even more effective. Thus, the customer-sensing team is an important tool for developing and executing strategy.

An early responsibility of this team is to define "customers." Too many companies define the "customer" as the distributor or the first organization to which the company actually sells. But that source is so removed from the real customer that it cannot provide reliable information for market sensing. For that we must turn to those who make the final buying decision and actually use the product.

The customer-sensing team wants to know who the real customers are and what they think and feel about the company's products and services and everything related to them. The team's goal is to draw insights that will help the company serve customers more effectively. There are several sources for this information: customer complaints; surveys of customer demographics, attitudes, and interests; focus groups of those who influence the buying decisions; company salespeople who sell to the customer; and even information from 1-800 numbers.

Another challenge is a word that cries out for insightful definition: "quality." Print and electronic media are swamping customers with that term without defining it. For example, does the "quality" of an automobile mean performance, reliability, durability, or all three? Without precise information, manufacturing people get inadequate information for making and improving the product; and marketing people work in the dark in making effective sales appeals.

Here are guidelines for seeking information from which insights about competitive factors may be drawn:

1. *Product performance.* A product with performance characteristics that are distinctive from those of competitors is often the most important competitive factor.

2. *Service factors.* Speed and reliability of delivery, packaging, and other service factors can be distinctive, competitive factors. Helping distributors and customers improve *their* profits falls in this area.

3. *Company/brand reputation.* Reputation for reliability of product performance and service can be a distinctive, competitive factor. A leadership company should have an inherent advantage here.

It has been said that "brands 'shout,' reputations 'whisper.' " The phrase is attention-getting but it also calls for thought. Many companies have many brands; each is costly to establish, and it is expensive to keep "shouting." If the company name and the brand name are the same (e.g., "Coca-Cola"), reputation also "shouts."

But reputation (without brand) must be built over time in many, many ways; and it can also be destroyed in many, many ways (e.g., by fraud and unethical conduct, which "shout" more than "whisper.")

4. *Price.* If none of the foregoing factors, individually or collectively, produce competitive advantage, the company must depend on price. Since price should always be the competitive advantage of last resort, the company must make continuous effort to keep *all* company costs at the lowest possible level, for example, by focusing on maximizing productivity.

Customers will typically be willing to help the company serve them better. They will provide information, but the sensing team must draw the insights. That team must then package its insights clearly for other leaders, and also encourage other leaders to work, personally, with customers in the field to develop additional insights.

Manufacturing Team. This network of leaders can help rescue manufacturing from its often functional isolation. My colleagues in McKinsey—and, of course, others—have come to see the importance of manufacturing as an integrated part of the total business, not something to be considered by itself. Too many companies tackle the manufacturing function expecting to reduce manufacturing costs by themselves—and that has led to belief in greater volume production and admiration for production lines.

In the early 1990s, Compaq Computer began pursuing its aggressive market-share strategy by slashing manufacturing costs deeply and consistently. The long assembly line was replaced by three-person "cells." In three years, Compaq doubled the number of PCs produced per square foot of factory space. The number of machines produced per worker jumped 50 percent. The higher production volume gave it greater clout to negotiate for price reduction in key parts like disc drives. Material costs attributable to volume discounts have declined 10 percent annually.[2]

Compaq says that the output of each person in the three-person cell increased another 23 percent, and that output per square foot of factory floor space rose 16 percent, compared to assembly lines.

Compaq believes that the real payoff from the work cell method will be to allow the company to build machines to customer order rather than forecasting what customers want. Matching production to customer orders reduces costs of every step of the retail and manufacturing network—inventory handling, freight, and unsold goods returned.

Compaq's strategy for achieving cost reductions was to crank up the volume of PCs it produced without investing in more factory space.

In a leadership company, the opportunities for the integrated cost reduction that Compaq brought about would be even easier to achieve because of its focus on the overall business and its greater flexibility.

In designing the subteams in manufacturing, it would be well to consider integration, as Compaq did, and reduce costs on an overall company basis, not in manufacturing alone.

Research and Development Team. In my view a leadership company would benefit more from R&D effectiveness than a command company for two reasons. First, since the objective of much R&D is to improve present products or develop new, related products, leaders in the network, with their broader understanding of the company, will be in a better position to make suggestions. Second, the network will be in a better position to help R&D commercialize new products to make them more salable.

In other words, the network of leaders—who listen with open minds and understand the company as a whole—can give more to R&D and get more from R&D, particularly when basic research is not the purpose of the R&D team. That does not mean the company should avoid basic research, but basic research is obviously so costly that the investment must be carefully evaluated, including the fit of the potential product with the existing line.

Supplier Team. Progressive companies are treating their suppliers differently today. The approach of driving down price through playing one supplier off against another is rapidly going out of style. The new approach is to treat suppliers more like *partners*—some companies even call them that. A few actually put them on teams. Some companies even let suppliers work on company premises,[3] but getting that close to suppliers requires care.

Fortune summarized the new approach: "Says a . . . top industrial manager: 'It's like committing to one relationship instead of sleeping around.' "[4] But there must be enough relationships to preserve competition and protect supply. Those that perform best are often given a larger share of the orders.

Close customer relationships help suppliers trim costs and improve quality by disseminating quality-enhancing techniques across company boundaries and by enlisting each supplier's technological expertise in helping to design and make new parts. Companies that succeed in making partners of suppliers usually set up the relationships routinely, not as exceptions. They also tie in suppliers logistically for ordering and handling inventories. They often split the savings.

A leadership company can readily tune in to this new trend by setting up a supplier team as a leadership team. The team leader does not need a price-oriented purchasing background. In fact, imagination and negotiating ability are more important. And the nature of company products may well determine what the background should be, for example, electronics, engineering, chemistry, or agriculture.

This team illustrates how many benefits can result from the creativity of team members who have the broad-gauged, open-minded attributes of leaders.

Advisory Leadership Teams

Technology Alert Team. In his book *Innovation,* my partner, Richard Foster, says, "The leaders in the current technology rarely survive to become the leaders in the new technology"[5] and that the attacker with the new technology has the advantage. The concept squares with my experience. Most companies are not as technologically alert as they should be and frequently fall prey to attackers; these may be present competitors (both direct and indirect), as well as new companies exploiting an old or a new technology.

With these and other forces of science, such as engineering and biology, at work, the rate of technological change has increased exponentially to become an explosion. In my view a leadership company, with its strategically positioned leaders, can inherently be more alert on all fronts. But to ensure that the technological front is protected and also ready to attack, I believe that nearly every leadership company, regardless of industry, should establish a technology alert team. For example, fast-growing retailers such as Wal-Mart gained competitive advantage by using many types of technology.

Hugh L. McColl, chairman of NationsBank, says that technology "is like a tidal wave. If you fail in the game, you're going to be dead." He adds, "We need a new strategy, and it's got to be a technology-based strategy." Now he has a team of 95 executives who track emerging opportunities and act as consultants.[6]

This team would *not* lead R&D; that is a separate and different operational activity. This team would have three types of responsibility: First, of course, to keep *defensively* alert to direct and indirect types of technological attack, and to bring them to the attention of the appropriate team. Second, to identify attack opportunities and then help R&D and marketing identify, commercialize, and improve related new products. Third, to ensure that the latest technologies are being applied internally to everything the company does. In fact, some companies have made "virtual attacks on themselves," by thinking through what competitors might do and defining what defenses the company might establish.

As you read the following passage from *Innovation,* consider whether the attackers or the defenders would have benefited from having a technology alert team:

> . . . Glass bottles, which helped Owens Illinois prosper, were replaced
> both by steel cans led by American Can and Continental Can and
> by paper cartons led by International Paper. Steel cans got their

comeuppance in the beverage segment from the aluminum cans of Reynolds Metals and Alcoa. Glass bottles for soft-drink beverages have given way to plastic bottles . . .[7]

The leader of this team and his or her few constituents would need, collectively, broad (not deep) related technological backgrounds, keen imaginations, unusual curiosity, and the capacity to envision what might happen.

Computer-Alert Team. The title of this advisory team requires explanation. The word "computer" is intended as a symbol for the electronic revolution that it started: mainframes, PCs, software, groupware, information technology, networks, videoconferencing, and so on. The word "alert" simply indicates that close watch must be given to this explosive field.

As I said earlier, there are not many leadership design specifics that will fit a wide variety of businesses; clearly this is one of them. Every company of any size will have a variety of computer and computer-related activities already under way. Nevertheless, this advisory team should be useful, and I offer it for consideration.

Computer and computer-type expenditures are typically so costly as to require top-management approval. And the explosive character of change in this field is likely to continue to require top approval. Most top managers do not have the technical skill to make sound judgments in this field; they even lack the time to keep up with consultants who, with professional independence, can advise them technically in making sound judgments.

The opportunities for valuable use of computers and related hardware and software are so great that none of the other teams should overlook them. Not only can computers cut costs directly through their operational use, but the information they supply can increase productivity through increasing sales and reducing costs and expenses. So an advisory team in this broad field can help other teams improve their performance. In fact, the computer-alert team may indicate that additional operational teams should be set up or that existing computer teams be reorganized.

Already, considerable work in the United States and elsewhere is being done through electronic networks, and there is more to come. The company's electronic network must, of course, be made part of the leadership design. Fortunately, the electronic network is easier to coordinate in a leadership company than in a command company.

Electronic networks break down or go around functional walls. "It's a welcome development, argues Robert Walker, chief information officer of Hewlett-Packard: 'With the ability to share information broadly and fully without filtering it through a hierarchy, we can manage the way we always wanted to.' "[8]

Sharing of information is valuable in a leadership company because so many people can use it. An electronic network should make it even easier to use in a leadership company, and on a global basis.

Network integration can speed product-development projects by as much as 25 percent, says Andy Ludwick, CEO of SynOptics Communications, a supplier of systems for electronic network integration.[9] And, properly run, electronic networks can enable a company to see its market more clearly.

In designing the electronic network to fit the leadership network, the possibility of overload of information should be borne in mind. Mark Rosenker, vice president of public affairs for the Electronic Industries Association, says, "E-mail is an incredibly valuable service, but when you become inundated, it gets to be just like junk mail."[10]

Another problem is the speed with which electronic networks are changing. Consider the PC alone: "Your prosaic office PC will evolve into a zoomy workstation. Among the payoffs: mind-boggling access to information from around the world and new ways to pool smarts with—and see—your colleagues."[11]

So the computer-alert team will be eternally busy keeping up with changes in computers and other elements of the electronic network. This team will also advise on the use of computers that are not part of the network. For example, computers may be used to do work that some other team is doing manually. In other words, this team provides other teams with overall information and advice on all phases of electronic information and how computers or other electronic devices can perform work that is now done manually.

This team would require a leader of stature with a high level of both technical knowledge and sound judgment. Of course, the level of knowledge need not be as high as outsiders might provide, but it should enable him or her (together with any constituents who might be needed) to stand up to outsiders and also to satisfy other team leaders and top management with the quality of the team's recommendations. Indeed, this team should also be qualified to convince other teams and top management that more information is being supplied than is needed.

The leader should also have time to keep up with the technical ability and professional independence of outside consultants who might be called on.

The present computer executive or chief information officer may be well enough qualified technically to become a leader and assume the role of leading this team, especially if he or she moves from an operational to this advisory role and is relieved of enough day-to-day administration. In fact, the chief information officer may perform the advisory role of the computer-alert team, and make it unnecessary to have such a team. But I believe it is important that the team have only an advisory role, rather than a combined operational and advisory role.

This design is feasible and effective in a leadership company because leaders are open-minded, not acting as rivals, and all focusing on the profitability of the company and the well-being of its people.

"Hustle Team." For this team title and concept, I'm indebted to Amar Bhide, Harvard Business School faculty member, McKinsey alumnus, and friend. In his perceptive article in the *Harvard Business Review,* "Hustle as Strategy," he says:

> Opportunities to gain lasting advantage through blockbuster strategic moves are rare in any business. . . . Countless companies in all industries, young or old, mature or booming, are finally learning the limits of strategy and concentrating on tactics and execution. In a world where there are no secrets, where innovations are quickly imitated or become obsolete, the theory of competitive advantage may have had its day. Realistically, ask yourself, If all your competitors

gave their strategic plans to each other, would it really make a difference?[12]

The hustle team has two responsibilities: (1) to coach leaders and teams in effective and efficient execution, concentrating on operating details, cost reductions, moving quickly, and getting things done right and on time (whereas in a command company they would be told and controlled); and (2) to provide logistical advice, especially in dealing with supply chains. Daryl White, chief financial officer of Compaq Computer, says that the company has already done most of what it needed to do to be more competitive: ". . . We've changed the way we develop products, manufacture, market, and advertise. The one piece of the puzzle we haven't addressed is logistics. It's the next source of competitive advantage. The possibilities are just astounding."[13]

Fortune tells how astounding the possibilities really are:

Last year American companies spent $670 billion—a gaping 10.5% of GDP—to wrap, bundle, load, unload, sort, reload, and transport goods. So clogged is the gross national pipeline with unnecessary steps and redundant stockpiles that the grocery industry alone believes it can wash $30 billion, or nearly 10% of its annual operating costs, out of the system. . . .[14]

Thus, the hustle team has a full plate of logistical opportunities and plenty of other things to do in coaching other teams.

The constituents of the team would be "modern" industrial engineers, that is, people who know how to achieve effectiveness and efficiency but can also sense ways to increase revenue.

Environment Team. "Since the celebration of the first 'Earth Day' some 25 years ago, the drive to improve the nation's air, water and land has come to occupy a secure place at or near the top of our national political agenda." So wrote Alfred C. DeCrane, Jr., former chairman of Texaco, in 1992.[15]

Since then, environmentalism has become a worldwide growth industry. Stringent laws have been passed in nearly every industrialized country. And environmental activists are eager to ensure that these laws are carried out, and that additional laws are enacted. For many companies the costs are substantial, and the outlook frightening.

Al DeCrane points out further that while virtually everyone recognizes the importance of protecting the environment, business has often put itself on the defensive. A national recession and two decades of experience with an endless flow of costly regulations have focused society's attention on economic realities. But environmental protection seems to spark an emotional response absent from most other public policy issues. People generally feel strongly about protecting the environment, and rightly so.

So every company must assess its environmental violations—actual and potential—and decide what it can do to deal with each particular situation. Some companies will find they have no problem or ones that can be easily dealt with.

But if enforcers of laws or activists allege company violations, or are likely to, I suggest that a leadership company establish an environment team to work with those company teams that are involved with the environment, to decide how serious the problems are, and to decide what the company can do to solve them.

Any company that faces these problems should not underrate their seriousness—and hence should have a knowledgeable team to deal with them.

Legal Team. A leadership company should have a legal team to advise the other teams on legal issues. The team leader should be the company's general counsel, and the number of constituents (and their legal qualifications) will depend on the nature, size, and complexity of the business.

Continuing changes in the practice of law in the United States will affect the makeup of such a team. In the past corporations typically retained law firms to serve as independent general counsel, and if that firm could not serve the company on a particular specialized matter, it would select another firm with the client's consent. Today, corporations may not have an independent (outside) general counsel; therefore, the company general counsel selects a specialized firm for each specialized matter that he or she cannot handle.

The legal team should encourage the other teams to consult it early, so as to avoid legal complications.

Strategy Team. Formulating strategy has long been the domain of top management. Top-level managers view themselves as the designers of strategy, architects of the structure to carry out strategy, and managers of the systems that direct and drive their companies.[16] That's the way it works in most command-and-control companies; in fact, in such companies strategy may be treated as a control factor as well as a performance guide.

In a leadership company, leading also comes from the top. The leader of the strategy team relates directly to a coordinator; but the leaders at the top will want all the help they can get from leaders throughout the company.

Network leaders and constituents will be qualified to contribute to strategy because they have a real stake in the company's present performance and future success, and an understanding of the business as a whole. Therefore, people throughout the company may have facts and knowledge to contribute to the development of strategy, intellectual as well as analytical. This broad participation should present a great advantage over the typical top-down development of strategy by a small analytical staff in a command company. Indeed, strategy can be formulated from the bottom up, as well as from the top down, with the chief executive and the coordinators meeting to reach final agreement on the strategy.

All this effort is worthwhile because, in a leadership company, strategy is taken seriously: The network teams implement the strategy they helped to develop.

The strategy team might well be assigned responsibility for developing and monitoring the company culture, making sure that, even in a leadership company, truthfulness and integrity are part of the culture. A well-designed strategy and a strong culture, combined, help to ensure a self-propelled company.

Since strategy in a leadership company is not a "control" device, there is no need to redo strategy every year—only when competitive conditions change (which may indeed be necessary before a year elapses).

Consider a sports analogy: In soccer the strategy is regularly changed as the team runs down the field. In American football the team usually stops while the strategy is changed, but occasionally a surprise running play is converted into a pass play. In business, the flexibility of a leadership company makes it better suited than a command company to a sudden change in strategy.

Each subsidiary and decentralized operating division would have its own strategy team, with coordination between and among parent and subsidiary units.

Review of conglomeration. As part of its initial work, the strategy team should decide whether to recommend eliminating subsidiaries, divisions, and strategic business units (SBUs) engaged in businesses that are unrelated to the core business. During the past decade, as CEOs were brought in to turn around faltering companies, they have typically been dumping such businesses, especially the popular finance and insurance companies acquired in hopes of shoring up core business profits.

Shortly after I joined McKinsey, I participated in an overall study of Marshall Field & Company, a major department store chain that had other businesses. I asked the president why he did not give more attention to a large division of poorly performing textile mills that manufactured products sold in Field stores, and that lost money. His honest answer was: "I never could understand why we bought those mills, and I'm just not interested in them." We recommended that they be sold, and they were. (These mills are still alive as a more successful separate enterprise selling to any buyer.)

After studying, observing, and participating in the conglomeration phenomenon for more than 50 years, I can find no guiding principle to suggest to the strategy team for acquiring noncore businesses. In cases where I could learn the real facts, the decision to make the acquisition seemed to be based on the personal opinion of the all-powerful chief executive, who usually rationalized his decision (none were women) by that seductive word "synergy."

Ever since that early experience, I have observed that the decision to buy or sell has turned principally on the "interest" (for whatever reason) of the chief executive. Of course, those were the days (and not very long ago) when the board was neither effective nor independent and went along with the CEO. In a leadership company, however, the chief executive will seek (or others will give) opinions of other company leaders and try to make an objective and sensible decision.

Of course, not all mergers or acquisitions are made to shore up weak earnings. I've participated in acquisition programs that have changed the basic character of the companies involved. Each made a series of acquisitions, all in another but related industry and each with a cultural fit. The programs worked out well, and the companies are still going strong.

As you can see, however, I'm skeptical about the success of acquired or merged companies *unless* there is a valid reason and a cultural fit.

A final responsibility of the new strategy team would be to decide whether strategic business units should be set up—whether SBUs headed by leaders might improve competitiveness and profitability. In a command company, SBUs are often set up so that the head of the unit can be compensated on the basis of unit profits and sized up for further advancement. In a leadership company, however, there would be no individual compensation based on unit profits, although there may still be competitive advantage for leadership companies to have SBUs.

I hope some of these cockshies may fit your particular company sufficiently well to provide guidelines in setting up your successful network of leaders. In any event, these example leadership teams illustrate that these are "working" teams: They don't just carry out strategic plans developed by top managers—they may well contribute to useful plans themselves.

EIGHT

Leading People to Like Their Work and to Adjust to the New Workplace

AFTER TALKING WITH PEOPLE about their work for more than half a century, I'm forced to conclude that most people in most command-and-control companies don't really like their work.

Why People Don't Like Their Work

I believe that a negative attitude toward work is inherent in command managing. The "superior" has inherent authority to put pressure on "subordinates" to produce better or faster results. Authority is easy to use, and most bosses use it. And most subordinates don't like it.

The term "boss" was once reserved for first-line supervisors, who usually treated their subordinates more harshly than most superiors up the line. This term has now spread up the line, all the way to chief executive. Business magazines, such as *Fortune* and *Business Week,* run feature stories on chief executives who are "tough bosses." Readers seem to like these articles because they zero in on truly tough bosses and are written with empathy for their subordinates.

"Who hasn't faced a boss's fury?" a *Fortune* story opened. "White hot or stone cold, it is hard to prepare for even when you know it's coming. Your brow moistens. Your gaze falters. Your gut flutters. Suddenly he is stomping with rage, and you are carpet."[1] Pollees in that story nominated more than 60 tough bosses; *Fortune* singled out 7 for rigorous criticism. The article continues: "So we define 'tough' broadly as 'demanding and hard to please, for whatever reason.' "

I know plenty of CEOs who are hard to please for any number of reasons. My observations or complaints include managers who push people tirelessly; are brutally demanding; publicly embarrass subordinates; set a crushing pace; fire people immediately if high targets are not met; leave people little time for their families; have a narrow focus that limits middle management, causing many to leave; and have big egos that subordinates must stroke a lot.

People Like to Be Led, Not Commanded

Does it take toughness on people for a company to be successful? I think not; in fact, the company will probably be less successful. Must people be laid off in order to increase share price? Certainly the CEO who is a leader, and other company leaders or leadership teams posted strategically throughout the company, will get much more help from constituents than most present CEOs get from intimidated subordinates because:

1. As leaders, they will treat people with fairness and consideration.

2. As leaders, they will build self-confidence, self-esteem, and spirit in constituents.

3. As leaders, they will focus on people as important individuals and constituents who are key to the company's performance and future success.

So it is my strong belief that a leadership company will be more effective partly because real consideration is given to people, motivating them so that, in working with others, they will do everything they can to improve company performance and will get personal satisfaction from doing so.

But, thus far, not many companies have accepted Douglas McGregor's Theory Y concept that people generally like to work (which, of course, does not mean that all people like their particular work). Indeed, most command companies inherently gear their policies, practices, and managing attitudes toward "making" people work. Of course, many managers are careful not to overuse authority, but many do not appreciate (recognize) how dispirited their subordinates feel under the pressure of authority.

When leading is substituted for authority, I believe most people will like their work, and that their enthusiasm for work will raise their performance to higher and higher levels.

People Policies for Leadership Companies

Leadership companies have policies designed to ensure that their people will be treated fairly and considerately. But there may be conditions that make layoffs impossible to avoid. In fact, for the past decade or two, the greatest fear people have had in going to work has been the threat of losing their jobs. There are, however, many ways that a leadership company can cushion the blows of layoffs.

Cushioning the Blows of Layoffs. For most people—and their families—being laid off is about the worst work-related development that can happen; it is sometimes compared to the death of a close relative. Layoffs affect not only those who have been laid off, but those who fear they may be laid off, and those who are concerned about their fellow employees at risk and their former fellow employees who are unemployed. Indeed, as I write in 1996, layoffs and the unemployment problem are much on the minds of most Americans. The problem goes way back and keeps returning.

With the recession persisting through the 1992 presidential campaign, the dark side of capitalism was dramatically displayed on television: people marching in the streets carrying signs and shouting, "We want jobs!"

Layoffs have been massive. "Nearly three-quarters of all households have had a close encounter with layoffs . . ."[2]

Even before the new CEO was brought in, IBM, well known for its lifetime-employment policies, had resorted to layoffs despite valiant efforts to avoid them. In June 1991, IBM's then chairman delivered an ominous message to employees over its electronic communications system. "IBM exists to provide a return . . . to the stockholders," and went on to quote Thomas Watson, Sr.: "The best and only assurance of personal reward and job security is to be part of a successful, prospering business."[3]

Thereafter, IBM continued a truly noble effort to maintain its tradition of no layoffs. At the 1992 annual meeting, the then chairman said: "By the end of this year, we will have reduced our population by more than 80,000 people from the peak year of 1986, eliminated 94,000 staff positions, 11,000 managerial positions, removed two layers of management, all without compromising our full employment, no layoff practice."[4]

IBM had avoided "compromising" by offering attractive early retirement packages that were widely accepted. But since the arrival of Lou Gerstner, who took office in April 1993, there have been additional layoffs.

The publication of two useful books that have an important bearing on cushioning layoffs will be helpful in custom-designing the network as we move through this chapter.

The New York Times Special Report *The Downsizing of America* (Times Books/Random House, 1996; hereafter abbreviated *Downsizing*) reports on the interviews of a *New York Times* team of reporters who, during the summer of 1995, interviewed workers, managers, and owners alike, to see how they have survived the economic storms that left a trail of anguish and upheaval. The interviews were expanded with research and published as a book in 1996.

The 100 Best Companies to Work for in America by Robert Levering and Milton Moskowitz (Currency, Doubleday, 1993, hereafter abbreviated *Best Companies*) looks at companies through the eyes of their employees. The book's primary purpose is to help people who are looking for a good place to work. The authors asked 400 corporate nominees for written materials showing why they should be considered, and selected 147 finalists for site visits from the overwhelming majority that responded. Among them: Anheuser-Busch, Armstrong, Compaq Computer, Dayton-Hudson, John Deere, Delta Airlines,* Goldman Sachs, Hallmark Cards,* Johnson & Johnson,* Merck,* J. P. Morgan, Motorola,* Northwestern Mutual Life,* Reader's Digest, Steelcase, Wal-Mart, and Weyerhaeuser. (* indicates that the company is among the ten best or five runners-up.)

Thus, *Downsizing* describes the layoff problems caused (in part) by command managing; and *Best Companies* describes how: "In a time of massive layoffs and cutbacks in benefits, . . . [these] 100 companies . . . have been able to maintain the people values that are the hallmarks of a good workplace—hallmarks that are not inconsistent with success and leadership in the marketplace."[5]

Downsizing says that one in ten American adults—or about 19 million people, a number matching the adult population of New York and New Jersey combined—acknowledged that a lost job in their household had precipitated a major crisis in their lives.[6]

There has been a net increase of 27 million jobs in America since 1979, enough to easily absorb all the laid-off workers, plus the new people beginning careers. And national unemployment is low. The sting is in the nature of the replacement work. Whereas 25 years ago the vast majority of the people who were laid off found jobs that paid as well as their old ones, Labor Department numbers show that today only about 35 percent of laid-off full-time workers end up in equally remunerative or better paid jobs.

Many Americans have reacted by downsizing their expectations of material comforts and prospects for the future. In a nation where it used to be a given that children would do better than their parents, half of those polled by the *New York Times* thought it unlikely that today's youth would attain a higher standard of living than their parents have. What is striking is that this gloom may be more emphatic among prosperous and well-educated Americans.[7]

In *Best Companies,* however, the companies profiled have handled their layoffs with fairness and consideration, recognizing that "there is nothing more traumatic than losing a job." Reasonable advance notice was given. Severance pay was generous. Employees were helped to find jobs in the company and/or on the outside. The authors say that the way layoffs are handled is their "litmus test" in company ranking. In their introduction the authors make these pointed remarks:

> There is more trust today [than in 1984, date of the first edition] because the authoritarian workstyle that has long been the standard operating procedure in American business has failed. It hasn't worked for employees, and it hasn't worked for employers. And that failure is at the root of the poor performance of American companies and the massive layoffs of the late 1980s and early 1990s. When management becomes disconnected from the people who work in

the company, it becomes easy to fire them. And when workers are disconnected from what they are doing, it becomes easy for them not to care about the product or service they're delivering.[8]

These books and other studies have convinced me that lack of companies to emulate in developing the leadership network is really no handicap. In fact, custom-designing a leadership network will, I believe, produce better results. Fitting the network to the specifics of each particular company will require creativity and experimentation; that should be better than emulating other companies anyway.

No company can foresee the future clearly enough to give employees an express or implied promise that if they do their work well they will be kept. (No company should even let employees assume there is such a promise.) Too much can happen. Technology can quickly make products or processes obsolete. Indirect competition may encroach or even take over. A competitor may develop a new strategy. Or there may be an economic recession or even a depression. Whatever the reason, when sales decline sharply, financial reserves can't usually last very long (not even GM's great resources) before paychecks or jobs themselves must suffer in order to preserve the enterprise itself. This is an inherent feature of capitalism. Jobs must die so that the company may live.

Downsizing says:

> . . . What distinguishes this age are three phenomena: white-collar workers are big victims; large corporations now account for many of the layoffs; and a large percentage of the jobs are lost to "outsourcing"—contracting work to another company, usually within the United States.
>
> . . . "I felt lousy about it," Arthur C. Martinez, Sears's chairman, said. "But I was trying to balance [50,000 eliminated jobs] . . . with the thousands of workers in our supplier community, and with 125,000 retirees who look to Sears for their pensions, and with the needs of our shareholders." . . .
>
> . . . some layoffs seem rooted in economic fashion. An unforgiving Wall Street has given its signals of approval—rising stock prices—to companies that take the meat-ax to their costs. . . . And

thus business has been thrust into a cycle where it is keener about pleasing investors than workers. . . .

The tally of jobs eliminated in the 1990s . . . has the eerie feel of battlefield casualty counts. And like waves of strung-out veterans, the psychically frazzled downsized workers are infecting their families, friends, and communities with their grief, fear, and anger. . . .[9]

However, profitable companies also make *strategic* layoffs. For example, as Procter & Gamble sought to cope with consumers' rising preferences for less expensive products, the company announced it would reduce its workforce by 12 percent within two years.

> . . . But while many corporate layoffs have occurred in troubled industries—from airlines to arms producers—Procter & Gamble is a healthy company in a profitable industry. . . .
>
> The elimination of 13,000 of 102,600 employees around the world might seem jarring, particularly for those affected and the communities where they live. But Procter & Gamble officials said the move was intended to make a strong company stronger and more capable of keeping its leading position among the manufacturers of household consumer products.[10]

Thus, many command managements are cutting people costs to increase profits and raise stock prices—*not* to preserve the enterprise.

Refusing to Treat People as "Disposables." The leadership company can have no "answer" to the layoff problem; it can only give greater consideration to people in its decision making. Companies are not in business to make jobs, but growing companies do create jobs. Therefore, leaders in leadership companies—in contrast to command-and-control companies—will feel that having created jobs, the company has a responsibility to the people who fill these jobs and to society: that is to run the company humanely and fairly so as to provide such job security as the company can afford. That will be caring for capitalism *and* people.

Thus, in all major decisions such as an acquisition, leveraged buyout, merger, alliance, or major expansion, the chairman and the board of a leadership company will weigh the decision carefully for its possible future impact on people. They will not avoid taking major risks, but neither will their decisions rest heavily on a layoff "cushion" should the deal not work out as expected.

Put another way, leadership companies will not use the possibility of future layoffs strategically; that is, they will not take corporate decisions and actions based on the assumption that people are "disposable." Indeed, leaders will regard executives who knowingly act as if people are disposable as unjust and inhumane. They'll understand that even those not laid off can become embittered, fearful, resentful, and unproductive.

Also, leaders will recognize a real danger: When hundreds of thousands of people throughout the country are treated casually as "disposables," capitalism as we know it risks further regulation.

These kinds of attitudes and assessments, which will permeate the leadership company—the board, chief executive, and the network of leaders—will help motivate everyone to improve company performance, the only sure road to job security.

Is downsizing slowing? Earlier I showed how serious downsizing has been. Now recognized authorities state that downsizing is slowing. But whether downsizing is increasing or slowing is not a controlling factor for a leadership company. Such a company treats its people fairly and humanely and so provides the best cushions that it can in its own financial circumstances at the time.

In other words, whenever layoffs are *necessary,* the controlling factor for the leadership company will be to do whatever is humane and fair, while avoiding the practice of using people to cushion decisions.

Cushioning examples. Here are specific cushions for consideration:

1. *Advance notice.* This is very important, and the longer the notice the better. It gives families time to adjust living expenses or decide to look for another job.

2. *Reduce compensation.* During the Depression, I had a personal experience with layoff policy that is still a relevant cushion. When all the banks closed, we young associates at Jones Day expected to get laid off since we knew the firm had two major bank clients. Instead, the firm sent out a notice that everyone, including partners,

would receive a 30 percent cut in compensation effective in two months. That would be the only cut. If further reduction proved necessary, only then would layoffs come. We young associates concluded that the policy was fair. Fortunately, no further reductions or layoffs proved necessary. (This was one deep cut with adequate notice.)

3. *Severance payments.* These payments usually vary with length of service.

4. *Early-retirement package.* This cushion, which takes many forms, has been used frequently in recent years.

5. *Training and education* for transfers to jobs within the company.

6. *Help in finding new jobs.* This policy is followed often in command companies, and would be expected in a leadership company. Some companies retain outplacement services.

Here are three examples from *Best Companies:*

Hewlett-Packard developed some unusual ways to cushion layoffs. HP was founded in 1939 by William Hewlett and David Packard, and the 1980s marked their gradual withdrawal. Most of all they had created an environment where the individual employee was valued. When people are declared "excess" for any reason, each has 90 days to find another job within HP.

If no job is found, the person's manager is responsible for finding one in any part of the country. If a person is offered a job within the same area (30-mile commute) and turns it down, the employee has the option of taking a severance package of one week's pay for every year of service, with a minimum of two months' pay.

If the employee turns down a job outside the present location, he or she has the option of a severance package of two weeks' pay for every year of service, with a minimum of four months' pay.[11]

John Deere is "the largest producer of farm machines like tractors and harvesters." In the 1980s, "the bottom fell out of the farm equipment business." The company encouraged employees to take early retirement but still had to lay off many others.

. . . The good news is that Deere survived the decade. . . . no mean accomplishment in an industry in which every other farm machinery equipment maker has either been merged, sold, or went bankrupt. But Deere didn't just survive the 1980s. They . . . made Deere a much better place to work. They entered new businesses, and instead of closing down factories, Deere kept all of them open, which earned them goodwill in the small Midwest towns where Deere has plants. . . . In recent years, the company has trained supervisors and assembly-line workers to work more cooperatively, which means lower-level employees now have more control over their work and supervisors have changed into coordinators. . . . Everybody is starting to listen to the people who are actually doing the job. Nobody knows better what they are doing than the person doing it. . . . Integrity is an important component of this value system. . . . *it's useful to keep in mind that the architect of the modern Deere was William Hewitt, a sophisticated San Franciscan who married into the Deere family and . . . ran Deere from 1955 to 1982, presiding over significant innovations in farm machinery and expansion of the company beyond the United States. . . .*[12] [emphasis supplied]

And the creative managing that Bill Hewitt initiated has carried on after his retirement. In their 1994 annual report Hans W. Becherer, chairman, and David H. Stowe, Jr., vice chairman, wrote that results showed that "a new Deere & Company is emerging. Our company today is marked by a spirit of continuous improvement, a determination to capitalize on positive developments in our worldwide markets, and a focus on profitable growth in each of our businesses."[13] Thus, the creative managing steps taken to "save jobs" resulted in a "new Deere & Company."

Johnson & Johnson. "There are not many jobs that are open. People just don't want to leave. . . . So if you want to work for a superbly managed company, head straight for New Brunswick"[14] (or one of the other of the 165 J&J family of companies).

And right here let me state the conclusion I drew from my study of these 100 companies: Although the authors selected and ranked companies on the basis of "people values" that are the hallmarks of a good workplace, I find that most of these companies are also outstanding in most other respects and hence can freely be called "well run."

This is clearly true of Johnson & Johnson. Most companies finish their letters to stockholders with a perfunctory thank you to the employees, which is unlikely to be very motivating. But J&J's Ralph S. Larsen, chairman, and Robert N. Wilson, vice chairman, *began* their Letter to Stockholders of the 1995 Annual Report by saying:

> 1995 was a great year for Johnson & Johnson—one of the best since the Company was founded nearly 110 years ago.
>
> The most important contribution to this excellent performance came from the creativity and dedication of the men and women of Johnson & Johnson—more than 82,000 strong across the world. We thank them for their hard work and extraordinary dedication to strengthening our competitiveness in a very demanding global marketplace.[15]

So rest assured that in designing a leadership company that will lead people to like their work, the leadership design team can, with confidence, select cockshies from a large number of progressive companies that focus on the well-being of their associates.

More Advisory Leadership Teams

Let's now carry on with more advisory leadership teams that I believe will also help people like their work.

Establishing a Health Team. A leadership company will want to provide high standards of health maintenance for executives and all associates, including annual physical examinations and advice on diet and exercise.

If the leader of the team is a physician, he or she will provide opportunities for company people to discuss health problems in strict confidence. Small companies could use outside consultants to give advice on diet and exercise.

Drugs. During the 1980s executives in a client company we had served for several years became concerned that workers were using drugs. We made a pro bono study: We believed we had been there long enough to have established trust with anyone we might interview about drug abuse—and that proved to be the case. Union representatives were pleased that we were making the study, and they cooperated thoroughly; so did everyone else.

Our most important findings were that drugs were being sold by outsiders in nearly every plant, and that some executives were using drugs.

More than a decade has passed. By now most companies should have organized drug abuse programs. However, no company that lacks such a program should assume that none is needed.

Establishing a Safety Team. Every leader will want safe working conditions for constituents, and constituents will require special knowledge depending on the nature of the risks they encounter on the job.

A good safety record will not only reassure company people about their work, but will be a factor in attracting new people.

Adjusting to the New Workplace

Most people will need to adjust to changes that come with conversion to a leadership company—changes I believe they will like.

Recruiting and Selection. A leadership company will need to recruit and select people carefully, whether potential leaders or constituents. Since McKinsey must recruit and select consultants with special qualities, you may find it useful to know how, and why, we go about it as we do.

A word of caution: Do not emulate what we do without careful thought. You will observe, for example, that our costs could easily be reduced. But recruiting and selecting consultants is so important to us and the loss of a trained consultant is so costly that we can't afford *not* to try to choose wisely.

First, we believe in recruiting only high-talent people, including minorities and women, all of whom will be given opportunities to advance, following a policy of meritocracy.

We combine recruiting and selection. Members of our professional staff conduct the interviews. Associates of usually one to three years' tenure conduct the first round of interviews. These are followed by additional interviews by longer-tenured people, and ultimately by partners, with unqualified candidates being dropped off along the way. Typically, a candidate is interviewed by about ten McKinsey consultants, and of course there is a great deal of individual judgment in the whole process.

We carefully define the qualities we are seeking and match them against candidate resumés and the attributes we discern in interviews. We seek only high-talent people, largely on the basis of education, scholarship, professional track record, and leadership activities. We also try to judge analytical ability, imagination, sensitivity to people, initiative, and drive. And we administer cases for testing problem-solving skills.

Our interviewers know our culture, and we believe it is important to the firm and to the candidates that there be a match. We try diligently to get good matches, but we aren't always as successful as we would like: Candidates may not like consulting work, and some don't measure up to our standards.

Also, like law firms and universities, we have an "up-or-out" policy: If our associates are not elected to partner within about six or seven years, we ask them to leave. We believe that is fair to them: High-talent people should find a field where they can be successful—and they do. I also believe it is unfair to "keep people on" when they lack the ability to progress. I believe this policy could be applied in a business if the action is taken soon enough and done fairly.

As to sources of candidates, we pioneered in employing candidates directly from graduate business schools and training them. Next, we began employing people for summer work between their first and second years of graduate business schools; this proved to be a good way of testing them and giving them a chance to determine whether they like, and do well at, our kind of professional work.

When a number of leading graduate business schools began requiring two years of experience before students could enter, it gave us a good opportunity to provide them two years of real experience, with no commitment by either party to join the firm after they complete graduate school. (We call them "business analysts.") In recent years we have received 5,000 to 6,000 resumés that indicate high-talent applicants, and the return rate after their graduation is quite satisfactory.

Gradually we sought high talent wherever we could find it—law schools, for example. Our latest source is Ph.D. graduates from various nonbusiness fields.

Then we have our own special business courses for training nonbusiness people, in which they have proven quick studies.

McKinsey and a leadership company have two qualities in common. First, we believe that good character ensures trustworthiness. We determine the quality of a candidate's character by interviewing him or her in sufficient depth by an adequate number of interviewers to make an ultimate judgment. Second, we need people who have the ability to work together effectively in teams. Since our interviewers will be working with candidates (although perhaps not this particular candidate), they make the judgment. (Some companies follow the practice of having candidates interviewed by the precise people with whom they will be working.)

Obviously, a leadership company should seek superior people: Talented, competent people working together in leadership teams can be real engines of growth, which will, in turn, attract more superior people. After his election to the National Business Hall of Fame in 1993, Thomas S. Murphy, the leader who built Capital Cities/ABC into a media giant before it was merged recently with Walt Disney Company, said: "If you hire the best people and leave them alone, you don't need to hire very many."[16]

Evaluation and Advancement. As a leadership company takes shape, a whole new approach to evaluating performance and advancement must be developed. No longer will getting ahead individually be a goal; stardom will be discouraged. A person's evaluation and advancement, including advancement to team leadership, will be based on his or her ability to work productively in leadership teams.

Of course, the company will need to develop entirely new ways to evaluate and promote people.

Job Rotation. In a leadership company, rotation is an effective way of strengthening teams. It helps people keep abreast in diversifying skills, and it broadens and deepens individual team members. Moreover, it helps counteract boredom. Rotation (even frequent rotation) just to relieve boredom should be characteristic of a leadership company.

Donnelly Corporation, manufacturers of windshields and other flat glass products, tells the new hire that "you are not being hired to do just one job." People work in teams, and everyone on each team is expected to learn all the jobs.

One Donnelly employee says: "The pride we take in our work reflects that we don't have to be necessarily supervised. We can actually function as human beings who have brains and we can sort of monitor one another." Donnelly workers are not displaced by technology; they are moved to another area, retrained, and integrated.[17]

Job rotation in a leadership company also increases the company's flexibility, because of the ease with which people can be transferred from one team to another. Transfers must, of course, take technical knowledge and skills into account.

Handling Work-Family Conflicts. Work problems and family problems never mix easily, although currently there is a mighty effort to overcome these difficulties. "The next frontier in the battle for higher productivity is shaping up to be in the arena of work and family," *Business Week* said in an editorial on such work-family problems as sick kids, elderly parents, and troubled spouses.[18]

Here, the leadership company has competitive advantages. When it comes to dealing with work-family conflicts, the evidence increasingly shows that the managers who get results are flexible rather than tough. Companies are helping employees resolve these conflicts through such arrangements as job sharing and compressed workweeks. "It's time for business to get in step with this country's evolving social patterns," says Continental Corp. CEO John Mascotte. "Corporate America can't afford to ignore or pay lip service to the work-family agenda anymore."[19]

This is not simply do-goodism. As *Business Week* points out:

Recent studies of such companies as Johnson & Johnson and American Telephone & Telegraph Co. show that helping employees resolve work and family conflicts boosts morale and increases productivity. The J&J study found that absenteeism among employees who used flexible time and family-leave policies was on average 50% less than for the work force as a whole. It also found that 58% of the employees surveyed said such policies were "very important" in their decision to stay at the company—the number jumped to 71% among employees using the benefits. . . .[20]

Yet many companies say that because of heightened global competition they can ill afford family-oriented programs, thus reflecting the short-term focus and inherent rigidity of the command-and-control system. Not so in leadership companies.

Training and Education. Leadership companies will want to train and educate everyone, including their hourly workforces. (The Bureau of Labor Statistics estimates that nearly two-thirds of the workers who will be in the labor force in the year 2005 are already on the job.)

By "training" I mean the development of skills for specific company tasks, and by "education" I mean broadening a person's knowledge and understanding for the benefit of the company and for the individual as well in all aspects of his or her life. Through continuous training, a leadership company can develop something of a permanent cushion against layoffs: When there are downturns in profits, people can be deployed in other company jobs.

Smart businesspeople realize that they, not the government, must take responsibility for educating their own associates in math, reading, and technical skills. Yet most companies don't offer worker training. Rather, they lavish their education budgets on managers and executives, short-shrifting the three-fourths of American workers who don't hold college degrees.[21] For companies progressive enough to convert to a leadership program this would not be so. Indeed, my bet is that these companies will find it profitable to train all hourly paid associates.

Some of the best training in America takes place at Motorola. Its factory workers study the fundamentals of computer-aided design, robotics, and customized manufacturing, not solely by reading manuals or attending lectures, but by inventing and building their own plastic knickknacks as well. The company runs its worldwide training programs from Motorola University, a collection of computer-equipped classrooms and laboratories at corporate headquarters in Schaumburg, Illinois.

In 1992 Motorola University, which includes regional campuses in Phoenix, Arizona, and Austin, Texas, delivered 102,000 days of training to employees, suppliers, and customers. This school doesn't employ many professional educators. Instead, it relies on a cadre of outside consultants—including engineers, scientists, and former managers—to teach most of its courses. Their role is to prod, guide, and orchestrate, not to pontificate.

> Motorola calculates that every $1 it spends on training delivers $30 in productivity gains within three years. Since 1987 the company has cut costs by $3.3 billion—not by the normal expedient of firing workers, but by training them to simplify processes and reduce waste. Sales per employee have doubled in the past five years, and profits have increased 47%.[22]

A leadership company could set up temporary teams to develop its own educational and training programs, calling on outside resources. Or development of the program could be handled by a permanent leadership team. "For American business, it all boils down to a singular lesson: If you don't train, you won't gain."[23]

Compensating People. Converting to a leadership company requires an entirely new plan for compensating people. No longer will they be compensated solely for individual performance, but largely for performance within a team. And that will be a big change.

Developing the plan. The drafting team for the new compensation plan should be a real operating team of seven or eight people from a cross-section of company activities—with perhaps two co-leaders, one each from personnel and finance. The co-leaders should be selected by the chief executive and the senior coordinators, and the co-leaders might select the other team members, with at least one member having been with the company no more than five years. That is only a cockshy for the team: Trustworthiness and good judgment are the chief criteria.

The assignment for the team should include monthly and weekly compensation, and should include profit sharing, then or later. The team should define its own task. A stockholder plan should follow later, and stock options should be considered.

Since McKinsey no longer provides consulting assistance on executive compensation, I can appropriately suggest that companies also consider retaining consulting firms that specialize in compensation. Such firms should have know-how that can be adapted to this new leadership situation, but, of course, their independence and objectivity should be verified. The company might restrict the consultants' contributions to "principles without numbers."

The leadership company would be seeking and developing superior people, so pay levels should be above industry standards. Developing new ways to pay people calls for creativity and experimentation.

Remembering that Sam Walton built the world's largest retailer in his own lifetime, let's go back to his book for guidance on compensation. Sam says that in the beginning he did not pay the employees very well. But as the company built more stores, each manager got a share of the profits of his or her store and so was a partner.

> But we really didn't do much for the clerks except pay them an hourly wage, and I guess that wage was as little as we could get by with at the time. . . . Back then, though, I was so obsessed with turning in a profit margin of 6 percent or higher that I ignored some of the basic needs of our people, and I feel bad about it.[24]

Later, Sam called the employees "associates" and treated them as partners. (This excerpt from his book is worth reading.)

> The truth is, once we started experimenting with this idea of treating our associates as partners, it didn't take long to realize the enormous potential it had for improving our business. And it didn't take the

associates long to figure out how much better off they would be as
the company did better. . . .

In 1971, we took our first big step: we corrected my big error of
the year before, and started a profit-sharing plan for all the associates.
I guess it's the move we made that I'm proudest of, for a number
of reasons. Profit sharing has pretty much been the carrot that's
kept Wal-Mart headed forward. Every associate of the company who
has been with us at least a year, and who works at least 1,000 hours
a year, is eligible for it. Using a formula based on profit growth, we
contribute a percentage of every eligible associate's wages to his or
her plan, which the associate can take when they leave the company—
either in cash or Wal-Mart stock. There's nothing that unusual about
the structure of the plan. It's the performance I'm so proud of. For
the last ten years, the company contributed an average of 6 percent
of wages to the plan. Last year, for example, Wal-Mart's contribution
was $125 million. Now, the folks who administer profit sharing—and
this includes a committee of associates—have chosen year after year
to keep the plan invested mostly in Wal-Mart stock, so the thing
has grown beyond belief, collectively, and in the individual accounts
of a lot of associates. Today, as I write this, profit sharing has around
$1.8 billion in it—equity in the company that belongs to our associate
partners.[25]

This is a striking example of learning leadership on the job. Sam's
admission of a "big error" was the mark of a leader. So was correcting
the error by starting a profit-sharing plan and involving associates in
administering it.

When the conversion to leadership stabilizes, I suggest that each
leadership company establish a profit-sharing plan and a program for
making everyone a shareholder. These mechanics alone won't get
results. Leaders at every level throughout the company must form
"partnerships" between their teams and the company. As Sam says:

It all sounds simple enough. And the theories really are pretty basic.
None of this leads to a true partnership unless your managers understand the importance of the associates to the whole process and

execute it sincerely. Lip service won't make a real partnership—not even with profit sharing. Plenty of companies offer some kind of profit sharing but share absolutely no sense of partnership with their employees because they don't really believe those employees are important, and they don't work to lead them. . . .[26]

I second that notion. Of the countless companies I have come to know and understand, not many treat their associates as truly important, although in the annual report the chairman usually talks about them that way. Some treat them miserably, even referring to them as "headcount." If the chief executive and other leaders are going to lead, they must believe in their people as constituents. We hear and read much about "lack of commitment and loyalty." Such dedication can't be "required" by command and control, but it can be earned through leading.

The CEO's compensation in a leadership company. This topic calls for special discussion, because the compensation of the chief executive establishes the level of others. The excessively high level of CEO compensation generally is one of the most publicized recent developments in the world of managing.

"Call it the year of the pay protest," the *Wall Street Journal* reported in 1992. "Presidential candidates and shareholder groups rail about too-high chief executive pay. Congress ponders ways to limit it, or at least make it more expensive for companies to offer it. The outcry has corporate directors 'on full red alert,' says Alan Ritchie, compensation vice president at General Mills Inc."[27]

In his remarkable book *In Search of Excess: The Overcompensation of American Executives,* Graef S. Crystal, Adjunct Professor of the Walter A. Haas School of Business at the University of California, Berkeley, concludes:

- U.S. senior executives are paid so far in excess of U.S. workers as to raise fundamental questions of equity, and even decency. And the gap is growing, not shrinking;

- U.S. senior executives are paid far in excess of their counterparts in the other major industrialized countries. And the gap is growing, not shrinking;

• U.S. senior executives are insulating themselves from pay risk to an alarming degree. In many companies, it seems as though there are almost no scenarios that could materialize to devastate the CEO's pay package, while there are an almost infinite number of scenarios that could materialize to enrich him.[28]

One common way to measure the level of chief executive pay (on which the pay of other senior executives is based) is to compare the inflation-adjusted total annual pay of the typical chief executive (excluding perquisites and fringe benefits) with the pay of the average worker. Using that approach, Crystal presents some striking findings on pay in manufacturing and lower-paying service industries:

1. Pay of manufacturing workers has been flat for 20 years, while CEO pay has risen more than three times.

2. While the typical CEO earned total compensation that was around 35 times the pay of an average manufacturing worker in 1974, a typical CEO today earns pay that is around 120 times that of an average manufacturing worker and about 150 times that of the average worker in both manufacturing and service industries.

3. During the past twenty years or so, the pay of the average worker, expressed in inflation-discounted dollars and adjusted for taxes, has dropped around 13 percent, whereas the pay of the average CEO of a major company (with the same adjustments) has risen more than four times.[29]

Crystal made a special study of 200 companies for *Fortune:* the top 100 industrials, the top 50 diversified service companies, and the top ten from each of the listings for commercial banks, diversified financial institutions, retailers, transportation companies, and utilities. Eighty-six percent of the CEOs of these companies earned $1 million or more per year, while the *average* CEO earned $1.4 million per year in base salary and annual bonus, and $2.8 million per year when the value of long-term incentives such as stock options was figured in.[30]

I agree that the U.S. senior executive pay system needs reforming—regardless of how companies are run: I believe the present system is harmful to U.S. business as an institution. But reforming the pay system is not a purpose of this book. My purpose in raising the excessive pay issue is to point out how it handicaps the chairman of a leadership company—and to suggest how top executive pay in a leadership company should be dealt with, not specifically, but in principle.

Converting to a leadership company may well require personal sacrifices by the CEO. And, as I have said earlier, the chief executive of a command-and-control company may not want to make those sacrifices, one of which is to forgo excessive compensation. Solving the excessive pay problem for the chief executive of a leadership company is very simple, but personally very painful.

If the CEO wants to be an effective leader of a successful leadership company, he or she can't accept excessive pay. Excessive pay will make people in the company feel that the chief executive is principally interested in self-enrichment and that he or she is not putting the business ahead of personal interests. These attitudes are demotivating to people in any company, but especially so in a leadership company.

Discussion of the excess pay issue is not confined to the business press—it makes headlines in newspapers and magazines and news on television. So it is unthinkable that the excess goes unnoticed by company people at any level. Unions, of course, shout about the excess and use it in negotiations. Nearly everyone in a leadership company will know when the chief executive and others at the top are receiving excess compensation. And they will feel that the senior executives are treating the rest of the people unfairly.

The senior executives of a leadership company must treat everyone in the company fairly, including themselves: that is the nature of leadership. The chairman and other senior executives must set the example. They are the role models. And with the spotlight glaringly on senior executive pay, they and the board of directors must use rare good judgment in determining what is fair compensation for themselves and then deciding what is fair for everyone else. (Some boards of directors are also sharing in the excess dollars and pension perks.)

So what *is* fair? Surprisingly, one useful guideline came from J. P.

Morgan at the end of the nineteenth century. According to Graef Crystal, Morgan decreed that chief executives of Morgan enterprises should not be paid more than 20 times the pay of the lowest-paid worker in the enterprise. And Crystal adds: "Most recently, Peter Drucker, the management philosopher from Southern California, . . . also opined that a CEO should not earn more than twenty times the pay of his lowest worker."[31]

But fairness can be determined only by the exercise of good judgment by the deciders, taking into account all the factors, especially the probable attitudes of the people who are receiving low pay. Decisions on bonuses, profit sharing, and stock option arrangements should be made in the same way.

In leadership companies, the very fact that they are establishing a new way of running the company suggests that senior executives are likely to be fair-minded in their decisions concerning their own pay: If they were intent on their own self-enrichment, they would not be trying to convert to this way of running the business. The command system is taking care of their enrichment very well.

Arch Patton, a recently deceased McKinsey partner who was a leading compensation authority before McKinsey left the compensation field, looked at it this way: "The easy availability of large sums of money seems to blur business judgment and make getting some of that money more important than self-respect."[32]

With Crystal's findings that current chief executive pay ranges from 120 to 150 times that of average worker pay, the Morgan and Drucker standard of 20 times will certainly not be popular with chief executives, nor will the 1974 manufacturing standard of 35.

Herman Miller, Inc., has a policy that restricts the CEO's pay to 20 times the *average paycheck* in the company, or $560,000 annually.[33] But it will not be easy for senior executives of leadership companies to set an example that will bring cheers from people at all levels and instill pride in their own companies without causing anger and shame from greedy chiefs of command-and-control companies. But biting the bullet will get easier after a few leaders set reasonable examples.

The Union Factor and the Law

Unions sprang up in the early part of the century and flourished because employees disliked the ways they were treated under the command-and-control system. They joined unions so they could deal collectively with their employers on pay, working hours, working conditions, work rules, safety, and other issues.

If negotiations were not satisfactory to the unions, they had the right to strike. And strike they did—with loss of life and injuries to both sides, and damage to company property. Thus unions fought their way to becoming an integral part of the managing systems of companies with which they had contracts.

Then the federal and state governments passed laws to protect the rights of unions, the rights of employees to join unions, and the way that union-company relations are conducted. Robert Reich, secretary of labor in the first term of the Clinton administration, wrote:

> . . . We have built up in this country since the 1930s a system of employment relationships, guaranteed by law and guided by business practices that have become norms. The state courts have essentially codified entire areas of workplace law having to do with everything from unjust dismissals through areas of labor-management relationships such as family and medical leave, which many of the states pioneered before the federal legislation was passed. Many people think this system needs fundamental rethinking.[34]

Thus, once a union contract has been signed, the union and the law become potent factors in managing the company. Managers have to consider not only the contract and the law but also the politics of working with the union on individual decisions. Two national unions merged so they could have more power, a goal they have achieved. And now a third national union is merging to gain further strength (that is, power).

But as managers began to administer the command system more compassionately, the need for union protection lessened and union membership declined. Currently, some government officials indicate that they will try to help the unions regain their strength.

This is not the place to go more deeply into union trends and issues. But from my consulting experience with many unionized companies—where I heard both sides of many issues—there are several considerations that, although fairly obvious, should be taken into account in deciding whether to convert from a unionized, command company into a leadership company.

1. In decisions to avoid or settle a major strike, the individual power of the chief executive is always a factor. (In some industries, wages have been racheted up by chief executives who wanted to avoid a strike before retiring, even when it was not good for the company.)

2. I am sympathetic with the past growth of unions because employees did need protection from managers who abused their command system authority, and some still do. However, I cannot believe there is a role for unions in a leadership company, for the following three reasons.

   First, a leadership company should not have an outside third party as an actual or "effective" participant in decision making. For example, to "score" and thus advance themselves within their own union hierarchies, union representatives and officers often try to wring unsound concessions from companies. That is a true conflict of interest. (Indeed, in union-controlled decisions I have observed, many were so harmful to the company's interests that they also severely hurt union members and union officers.)

   Second, in heavily unionized companies, managers seldom make a major decision without asking themselves or their bosses how the decision might affect union attitudes. I have observed many companies drop important productivity improvement opportunities without even discussing them with union representatives, because they believed the union would oppose them.

   Finally, in current union negotiations, union attempts to preserve jobs are looming large.

For these reasons, I believe that—for the near future—unionized companies face a virtually impossible task in converting to leadership companies. Before chief executives and boards of directors take on conversion struggles with unions, good judgment dictates that they wait for nonunion companies to set successful examples as leadership companies.

Responsibilities to One Another

I believe that in a leadership company most people will like their work. But the company will be an even more enjoyable place to work if the culture is designed to make it that way.

Leading fosters a working atmosphere that stimulates an open exchange of ideas and fosters dissent. People should show a genuine concern for one another and treat one another with fairness, as peers and friends.

With such an atmosphere it should be a pleasure to come to work.

NINE

Corporate Governance for a Leadership Company

WHEN WILLIAM J. AGEE, then the all-powerful chief executive and chairman of Morrison Knudsen Corporation, giant construction and transit equipment company, convened a board meeting in February 1995, he was immediately asked by the other directors to leave the room. A few hours later, two directors told Agee that he was fired as chief executive officer, president, and director.

This unusual action was closely covered by the *Wall Street Journal* and the *New York Times* because it was representative, although certainly not typical, of much board performance under command-and-control managing during the 1980s and 1990s. The *New York Times* reported:

> By now, the lesson is clear to every chief executive in corporate America: build friendly relations with your company's big shareholders or else. All the stormy C.E.O. departures at major corporations in the last few years—General Motors, I.B.M., Eastman Kodak, Morrison Knudsen and others—have followed much the same script. Performance lags, the stock-price languishes and the major shareholders apply pressure to the board of directors, who then oust the hapless chief executive.[1]

Agee's ouster was the last act in a sharp about-face by a board that, with one exception, began 1994 as a complacent group of hand-picked Agee friends. The board's immediate decision was made as a result of pressure from bank lenders.

In the six years that Agee ran the company, he failed to develop steady growth in operating profit. He also left the corporate headquarters in Boise, Idaho, and tried to run the company from his home in Pebble Beach, which abuts the famous golf course. As problems and complaints about his management developed, employee morale sank, the stock price fell, unexpected quarterly losses were reported, and an even larger loss was later announced. And still later (June 1996) the corporation took bankruptcy.[2]

At its long ouster meeting the board did not take up the matter of Agee's separation compensation, but the *Journal* followed up promptly with an article on that aspect of the saga.[3] For instructive examples of inaction and bad judgments by ineffective boards of major companies, the following passage from the *Journal*'s account of the Agee separation compensation is worth reading:

> Under his 1991 employment agreement, the ousted chief executive [Agee] could collect a minimum of $1.23 million a year for two years, concludes an analysis conducted for *The Wall Street Journal* by Executive Compensation Reports, a Fairfax Station, Va., newsletter. The total of at least $2.46 million far exceeds Mr. Agee's 1993 base salary of $750,000. . . .
>
> Mr. Agee has collected handsomely before from a company he has left. Indeed, he was the first chief executive officer of a major company to collect a "golden parachute." He walked away with $3.9 million over five years when he resigned from Bendix Corp. following its acquisition of Allied Corp. (now AlliedSignal Inc.) in 1983. Critics contend that such "golden parachutes," offered to managers who leave in the wake of a takeover, waste corporate assets. . . .
>
> If Mr. Agee succeeds in winning his full severance pay from Morrison Knudsen, it will mark his second handsome payment for a corporate fiasco, according to Judith Fischer, publisher of Executive Compensation Reports. . . .
>
> "It must be nice to be a CEO," says Nell Minow, a principal at Lens Inc., an activist investment fund in Washington, D.C. It's one of the few jobs in America, she adds, "where you get paid for failure."[4]

For companies shaping up their governance, the lessons from the Morrison/Agee fiasco should not be ignored.

Corporation and Board Relationships:
The Critical Connection

John Pound, member of the law faculty and chair of New Foundations, Harvard University's multidisciplinary research project on corporate governance, concludes that at its core, corporate governance is not about the power struggle between management and the board; it is about their working together to ensure effective decision making.[5] Pound says:

> Ultimately, what is needed is a system in which senior managers and the board truly collaborate on decision making. In addition, both directors and managers should actively seek the input of institutional shareholders. Institutions are no longer the passive constituents of the managed-corporation model; they have emerged as serious players in the governance process.[6]

Pound says further, ". . . most performance crises are the result of errors that arise not from incompetence but from failures of judgment."[7] True. But for all the reasons we have discussed in these pages, judgments brought to the board by leaders are likely to be better than those coming to the board in a command company. Moreover, the effective working relationship between leaders and directors in a leadership company further ensures the exercise of sound judgments for such momentous decisions as passing on acquisitions.

Specific policies (as guidelines) for running the business are what matter to the board, and one of the real problems is the board members' unwillingness to challenge specific policy decisions. Directors are more likely to offer challenge once they are convinced that leaders and directors are working together to make the best possible decisions and that on appropriate issues major shareholders will also have a voice. Leaders with open minds will welcome that challenge. The goal of both would be to minimize the possibilities of mistakes and to increase the speed with which they are corrected.

The Campbell Soup Co. management and board have developed (and made public) progressive corporate governance standards that require management and the board to work together. For example, standard 4 states: "Every year the Board will review and approve a three-year strategic plan and a one-year operating plan for the Company."

But U.S. companies generally have a long way to go to achieve effective working relationships between managements and boards. The purpose of this chapter is to outline the forces at work and to suggest how managements and boards can cope with these forces through working together for the benefit of the company.

The power struggle between CEOs and their boards. The record shows that over the years relations between most all-powerful CEOs and the boards of command-and-control companies have ranged from CEOs simply ignoring the board to their struggling to wrest power from the board.

Decades back, when inside directors dominated boards, the CEO could ignore the board. Also, when they put their friends on the board, CEOs could have their own way. Various pressures have largely corrected these serious problems. But a high proportion of directors are still toothless and listless watchdogs, although "watchdog" describes only a part of the director's role. Still, institutional shareholders have not been idle.

New Forces at Work

Beginning in 1987, Dale M. Hanson, CEO of the $80 billion California Public Employees Retirement System (CalPERS), began fighting for management accountability and boardroom reform of poorly performing companies whose stock CalPERS held. After a slow start in getting CEOs and outside directors to meet with CalPERS, Hanson became "America's most prominent activist shareholder," according to a 1994 article in *Business Week*.[8]

In planning the attack, Hanson worked with CalPERS general counsel, Richard H. Koppes. Hanson "met with . . . CEOs of 56 companies and held many talks with outside directors." According to *Business Week*, CEO Bruce Atwater of General Mills said, "Dale has won great respect in the corporate community."

Business Week's article went on to say that "Hanson was in the thick of headline-making battles at Westinghouse, Sears, American

Express, IBM, Advanced Micro Devices, and Time Warner, plus many more events behind the scenes."

Smaller investor forces are also at work.

> Shareholders cannot vote "no" to unopposed directors. They can only abstain by withholding their support. . . . For example, at the 1993 Westinghouse annual meeting, Robert A. G. Monks . . . was able to announce that his firm's $3 million holding represented more stock [than that] held by the entire board of directors put together, and nearly three times more than [that of] all the outside directors . . . put together. . . .[9]

All-powerful chief executives, who sit at the top and command the situation, can stay at the top until their boards lose confidence in them and decide to remove them. In other words, the debate over governance has centered on power, and of course some chief executives still want their friends as directors, and they often succeed. But removal of the chief executive by one board strengthens the resolve of directors of other boards to follow. So a bandwagon effect for change is developing.

Let's add one more example to the bandwagon: the case of W. R. Grace & Company, the $4 billion specialty chemical and medical services company, discussed in a *New York Times* article, "Big Investor Talked, Grace Listened." The Grace boardroom shakeup in March 1995 is seen as a watershed in the annals of corporate governance.

Instead of taking on a company that was performing poorly, Teachers Insurance and Annuity Association-College Retirement Equity Fund decided to push Grace (which was doing well) to do better. That was a significant shift in emphasis: TIAA-CREF—the world's largest pension fund, with more than $66 billion in stocks alone—asked for better results. Robert Monks was quoted as saying, "In the case of Grace, what has happened here is really important. . . . CREF is creating the correlation between governance and value. They have a lot of money invested in the company, but a lot of money in Grace hasn't been made yet. They became involved in order to make money. Ultimately, trustees at other pension funds are all going to have to look at governance the same way."[10]

In recent years pension funds have increasingly sought to put pressure on underperforming companies, most recently at Kmart. What TIAA-CREF did with Grace is a further refinement. One can almost hear the bandwagon effect of the Grace response.

The implications could be far-reaching, because as a way of increasing value for its 1.7 million participants, TIAA-CREF has initiated a program that intends to broaden its scrutiny of companies already in its portfolio. John H. Biggs, TIAA-CREF's chairman and chief executive, says, "Our new program involves systematically looking at the corporate governance practices of our portfolio holdings."[11]

As a result of these developments, two bandwagons are rolling: Corporations are making governance changes voluntarily, and pension funds are pushing other corporations to do the same. But I urge pension funds not to push so hard that chief executives will focus on short-term strategy and decision making, that is, on pushing for current higher stock prices. Directors should be watchdogs against short-term thinking, and wise executives of pension funds will support directors in the interest of greater long-term profits on their investments.

These watershed changes in the governance of command-and-control companies are gradually giving boards more control over CEO decisions. Clearly, there needs to be a change in CEO attitude toward the role of the board—not a legal change but a working change. What is needed is a board that will be a mentor as well as a monitor. And such a board requires members whose qualities are trustworthiness, independence, competence, judgment, courage, and real interest in the business.

General Motors' Contribution

Early in 1994, John G. Smale, retired CEO of Procter & Gamble and then nonexecutive chairman of General Motors' board, took the initiative in leading GM's other outside directors and a team of assistants in developing new board guidelines for GM.

The new GM guidelines, together with the way that Mr. Smale ran the board meetings, have produced constructive, open discussions in the meetings. And directors are getting deeper into GM's business. Harry J. Pearce, then GM general counsel and now vice chairman, who has attended board meetings since 1987, said, "The difference is night and day. . . . Everyone can speak candidly, there's no sense of not wanting to hear something, and it doesn't matter if it's controversial. . . . They're getting more complete, more detailed, more relevant information, and they're asking tough questions that enable us to do business better."[12]

Certainly that's the way a leadership company would want its board meetings conducted—indeed, *any* company should want its board meetings conducted that way. Only in that way can the board and the management have an effective decision-making relationship.

Mr. Smale and GM have performed an important service to the business community (and thus to society) by making the guidelines public.* The guidelines were revised in August 1995, and with GM's permission, I have included them as Appendix B for the reader's convenience so I may comment on them. Although I don't agree with all of them, I do agree with *Business Week* when it said: "Every board in Corporate America should sit down, review GM's practices, and see if their conventions measure up."[13]

Following that advice, I've reviewed the Harvard-based research and GM guidelines to determine whether, together, they will serve most companies, both command-and-control and leadership.

I've also had the good fortune of learning the British viewpoint on corporate governance from Hugh Parker, a retired McKinsey partner who practiced in our New York office until 1957 when he transferred to open, and lead, our London office. He developed a special interest in board governance, and wrote *Letters to a New Chairman*, a monograph published by the (British) Institute of Directors in 1979 which he updated in 1990, with the assistance of 16 British chairmen.

Since his retirement from McKinsey in 1984, Hugh has served on several British and American corporate boards and continued his study of corporate governance. Thus, for more than 25 years Hugh has studied and written about corporate governance on both sides of the

---

*John Smale was inducted into the National Business Hall of Fame in April 1996, based on his contributions to Procter & Gamble *and* General Motors. One commentator on the election said, "Smale would have been a shoo-in for the Hall of Fame on the basis of his first career."

Atlantic. Few others have his breadth and depth of knowledge of corporate governance. Thus we have a third source on which to draw.

Importance of a Corporation

We in the United States must always remember Chief Justice William Rehnquist's 1978 opinion that "A state grants a business corporation the blessing of potentially perpetual life and limited liability to enhance its efficiency as an economic entity."[14]

Indeed, every corporation is an important "economic entity" for these reasons: (1) it provides goods and/or services for people, (2) it provides jobs and wealth for its employees, (3) it creates wealth from investments by shareholders, and (4) collectively, corporations largely determine the standard of living for the nation. Therefore, it is important (even to the nation) that every corporation be an efficient economic entity.

The board of directors is given the right and obligation (by law) to protect the "blessings" of "perpetual life" and "limited liability." But "to enhance its efficiency," the board of a corporation has great responsibility.

Comments on Conventions

And now some comments on conventions, drawing principally on GM guidelines, Parker, and, to some extent, on the Harvard-based research. Since the GM guidelines are available in Appendix B, I call attention only to those that are new or important and the few with which I disagree.

Responsibilities of a Board. The most important new material in the GM 1995 Corporate Governance Guidelines, in my opinion, is this opening statement of the mission of a board of directors.

> The General Motors Board of Directors represents the owners' interest in perpetuating a successful business, including optimizing long term financial returns. The Board is responsible for determining that the Corporation is managed in such a way to ensure this result.

This is an active, not a passive, responsibility. The Board has the responsibility to ensure that in good times, as well as difficult ones, Management is capably executing its responsibilities. The Board's responsibility is to regularly monitor the effectiveness of Management policies and decisions including the execution of its strategies.

In addition to fulfilling its obligations for increased stockholder value, the Board has responsibility to GM's customers, employees, suppliers and to the communities where it operates—all of whom are essential to a successful business. All of these responsibilities, however, are founded upon the successful perpetuation of the business.

If the chief executive in a company performs poorly and the directors do nothing, everyone suffers economically: employees who are downsized (and their families); shareholders; the community; and, collectively, the nation as a whole.

. . . the period from September 1992 through December 1993 appeared to be an open season on chief executives. The CEOs of General Motors, Westinghouse, American Express, IBM, Eastman Kodak, Scott Paper, and Borden were all pressured to resign in the face of their companies' long-term underperformance. These moves were heralded in the media as a breakthrough in boardroom activism. Yet in all these instances the board took the necessary drastic action years too late. . . . Why does it take boards so long to respond to deep-seated competitive problems? And, if one of the leading responsibilities of directors is to evaluate the performance of the CEO, why do boards wait too long for proof of managerial incompetence before making a move? . . . Boards of directors are the "watchers" who govern the destinies of today's corporations.[15]

In his article, Pound gives an example of Westinghouse.

. . . by the late 1980s, there were clear internal warning signals about the company's aggressive move into financial services: great risks were being taken by a relatively inexperienced divisional team. The move was allowed to continue and expand until, in the early 1990s, it blew up and dragged the company into disaster. . . .[16]

If the Westinghouse directors at the time had been independent and had challenged the entry into the new field or had insisted on leaving the field earlier, the financial services disaster would not have continued to plague the company. This is an excellent example of the importance of having an independent and effective board to ensure that the corporation is an efficient economic entity.

Inside/Outside Director Mix. The importance of a predominance of outside directors has now become well established among American companies. Among Fortune 100 companies in 1991, the average number of insiders was 3.39 and the median number was 2.76. By 1995, the number of *insiders* had declined so that the average number was 2.80 and the median was 1.92.[17] This sharp downward trend in number of insiders reflects pressures of many types that make up a market.*

Introducing Potential Directors. Some boards have followed the practice of putting all possible candidates for future CEO on the board so outside directors can size them up. That practice has led to raising the hopes of senior officers by making them directors unnecessarily.

GM guideline 7 deals with that hope by saying, ". . . The Board is willing to have members of Management, in addition to the Chief Executive Officer, as Directors. But, the Board believes that Management should encourage senior managers to understand that Board membership is not necessary or a prerequisite to any higher Management position in the Company. . . ." In my opinion, it is better to fix on a small number and omit the explanation.

Executive Committee. GM's Guidelines do not provide for an executive committee although they do not explicitly exclude it. When a company has an executive committee, its activities should be sufficiently routine so that other directors will not feel they are serving on a "two-tier" board with a small number of directors making decisions for the whole board.

---

*On matters of corporate governance, GM guideline 7 specifies that decisions will be made by the outside directors.

As of January 1, 1996, Mr. Smale stepped down from his post as chairman, and the board established a new executive committee that Mr. Smale is heading. He also became the "lead director," coordinating management oversight and serving as chairman of three yearly meetings of GM's outside directors. At the same time the board named John F. Smith, Jr., the president and chief executive, to the post of chairman, and elected Harry J. Pearce, an executive vice president, to the board and elevated him to vice chairman.[18]

Committee on Director Affairs. About half the companies listed on the New York Stock Exchange have nominating committees. GM has placed this and other responsibilities on the Committee on Director Affairs (CDA)—another good idea to come out of GM's study of corporate governance.

Annually, the CDA reviews (with the board) the appropriate skills and characteristics that the board requires in the context of the current makeup of the board, which includes diversity, age, background (such as understanding of manufacturing technologies), international background, and so on. This review defines the board's perceived needs for new directors and the qualifications of those directors.

Guideline 15 makes the CDA also responsible for an annual assessment of the board's own performance. This new and useful guideline says:

> The Committee on Director Affairs is responsible to report annually to the Board an assessment of the Board's performance. This will be discussed with the full Board. This should be done following the end of each fiscal year and at the same time as the report on Board membership criteria.
>
> This assessment should be of the Board's contribution as a whole and specifically review areas in which the Board and/or the Management believes a better contribution could be made. Its purpose is to increase the effectiveness of the Board, not to target individual Board members.

The financial decline of corporate giants has set off a wave of pressure on big companies to yield more power to outside directors, and this, in turn, has led boards to establish new kinds of committees. I believe the CDA can cover a range of useful activities, thus minimizing the need for additional committees (and more meetings).

Formal Evaluation of CEO. There should be a formal evaluation of the CEO annually. (In a leadership company, the chief executive would also welcome informal suggestions on how his or her performance can be improved.)

Guideline 26 states: "The evaluation should be based on objective criteria including performance of the business, accomplishment of long-term strategic objectives, development of Management, etc.," and "will be used by the Executive Compensation Committee in . . . considering the compensation of the Chief Executive Officer."

Executive Compensation Committee. This committee has a tough role in these days of excessive compensation at the top. I have already expressed my view that the chief executive and other senior executives in a leadership company should not accept compensation that people in the company would feel is so excessive as to be unfair. But chief executives of command-and-control managed companies should also be ashamed to accept excessive compensation, particularly when the company is faltering and laying off people.

Outside directors have a key role here. After meeting alone, outside directors should try to persuade the chief to take reasonable compensation (or insist that he or she do so)—even if that means accepting lower compensation than the chief's peers are getting in other comparable companies, as reflected in compensation rankings published in business magazines.

Critics of excessive executive compensation recommend that it be related more closely to performance. Other boards are likely to follow GM's fair and sensible guideline, which calls for a formal evaluation of CEO performance annually.

GM is following its own guidelines concerning performance. The company earned a record profit in 1995; but because results fell short of aggressive targets set by the board, salary and bonus payouts to top executives were cut. For John F. Smith, Jr., GM's chief executive, that meant a cut of 9.2 percent from 1994, and for the next three most senior managers of 6.5 percent.

Mr. Smale, who still heads the executive compensation committee, was paid $200,000 in 1996, down from $500,000 in 1995. "He relinquished the chairman title . . . but he still has somewhat more responsibility than a regular director on the board," said a GM spokeswoman.

" 'It's terrific to see. It's unusual to find a company that walks the talk,' said Robert Salwen, a principal of Executive Compensation Corp. . . . 'I think GM is fast becoming a bellwether company in the area of corporate governance.' "[19]

I can't prove it, of course, but I feel sure that the published compensation rankings are a contributing factor in the current excessive levels of executive compensation. Chiefs, understandably, don't like to feel they are paid less than their peers in their industry, and such comparisons give compensation consultants a "justification" for suggesting raises for chief executives and senior management. Thus, publicity produces a subtle upward ratcheting of chief executive compensation, which spreads to other senior executives and to other companies.

The executive search firm seeking a new CEO can also ratchet chief executive compensation upward. Compensation is, of course, an important factor in motivating an individual to move from one company to another, and in "making the market" for the position, the search firm can easily "raise the ante." In its decision-making role, the board can help ensure that this so-called market is a truthful and sensible one.

In a list of "22 Questions for Diagnosing Your Board," Harvard Business School's Walter J. Salmon asks: "Has your compensation committee shown the courage to establish formulas for CEO compensation based on long-term results—even if the formulas differ from industry norms?"[20]

If the board retains compensation consultants, those consultants should not report to anyone in management, only to the compensation committee, thereby making it less likely that they will be perceived as "buttering up the boss." (I'm pleased that McKinsey gave up our compensation consulting practice many years ago. Our people involved in that practice felt there was a conflict of interest, and that we could not be perceived as being disinterested in CEO compensation.)

Also, the compensation committee (of any company) should approve the new compensation plan that the management would have to develop for a leadership company.

Separating the Roles of Board Chairman and Chief Executive. When the chief executive of GM was removed toward the end of 1992, the board advanced the president to chief executive and elected Mr. Smale chairman of the board. These actions took place after a long period of board passivity and signaled that the board was now ready to discharge its responsibilities.

However, GM guideline 4 says that the board does not have a policy on separation but leaves the decision to the judgment of the board. Here I differ with the guideline. I agree with Hugh Parker, who is convinced that if a company chairman is also the CEO it is impossible for any board to fulfill its independent role of monitoring the CEO. Hugh says, "The main purpose [of the separation] . . . is to restore a healthier balance between quite different roles of an effective board of directors under the leadership of an independent chairman, and of the company's management under the leadership of a capable CEO."[21] He believes that in the United Kingdom over 80 percent of public companies have separated the roles, and he expects it to approach 100 percent by the year 2000. Hugh puts it this way: "A strong and effective board can only be so under the leadership of a strong and *independent* chairman."[22]

Hugh writes further: "What seems to have happened in the U.S. is that, by tradition and by natural inclination of capable and strong-willed CEOs, the very title [of chairman] has become invested with dangerously large powers. When the title of chairman is also subsumed with that of CEO, these powers can become virtually absolute,"[23] reminding us of Lord Acton's axiom: "Power tends to corrupt and absolute power corrupts absolutely." I have seen that happen in chief executives. That's why I have referred often to the "all-powerful chief executive."

When Mr. Smale relinquished his post as chairman, he went on the record for the first time with his thoughts about governance when he gave an interview to the *New York Times*. He gave three reasons for transferring the chairmanship to John F. (Jack) Smith, the CEO, and becoming lead director himself. ". . . [T]he board felt that we should not institutionalize the idea of nonexecutive chairman . . ." Mr. Smale felt that Smith had made tremendous progress and that it would be unfair to Smith for Smale to retain the title until he (Smale) reached 70. (He was then 68.)

> And the other factor is that I wanted to back away from the amount of time I was spending on this. And there was no easy way to [do] that and do the job as chairman, given the way I approach what I do. . . .
>
> I won't be chairing the board meeting; Jack will. I generally gave the board my thoughts about the subject we were talking about, and I'll have to figure out how and whether to do that in the future. I'll do that, but more likely it will be in response to questions from other directors. . . .[24]

What Mr. Smale says about the separation of chairman and CEO depending on personality and time available makes sense. But I still believe that if someone fits personally and has the time, a separate chairman from outside the company will, as some GM shareholders felt, "instill greater management accountability."

As another *New York Times* article expressed it:

> . . . the change is a setback to the corporate governance experts and shareholders who believe that splitting a company's top job adds a measure of executive accountability that over time leads to better performance. "It's unfortunate," said Richard H. Koppes, deputy executive officer of the California Public Employees' Retirement System, the huge pension fund that helped precipitate G.M.'s executive changes in 1992. "This is no comment on Jack, but we think these positions should be separate."
>
> Mr. Koppes has plenty of company. A recent survey of 240 institutional investors by Russell Reynolds Associates, an executive recruiting firm, found that 54 percent preferred that the jobs of chairman and chief executive be held by two individuals. Yet by most estimates fewer than 10 percent of the nation's companies use that structure,

and it is viewed by executives mainly as a temporary option for troubled companies.[25]

I do hope that companies overhauling their governance guidelines will separate the board's top job—chairman of the board—from president and chief executive, thus providing the board the opportunity to join with the president in decision making on major issues. (Suppose a Westinghouse chairman in the 1980s had required the president to discuss with the board entering the finance field.)

Selecting Director Candidates. A board cannot be independent unless its members have independent or disinterested viewpoints. And this is more difficult to measure than competence.

I believe that "disinterested" or "perceived to be disinterested" is the clearer test of independence; consider company lawyers, bankers, investment bankers, consultants, or advisers of any type, including professors. In McKinsey, we considered all aspects of this issue in developing our policy that no active member of our firm shall serve on a corporate board.

Indeed, I believe it is wise to extend the definition to include people who may be motivated to hang on to a directorate, such as a retired CEO who might want to keep a directorate for something to do, for companionship, for an attractive flow of cash, or for the perks. That is why the committee should try to learn as much as it can about the candidate's motivations for wanting to serve, and to the extent possible, the likelihood that he or she will make and keep a commitment to being independent. (A separate chairman of the board could help strengthen "wavering" directors.)

Former CEOs as Board Members. Guideline 9 says this is a decision to be made in each individual instance. I do not agree. In my opinion, the retiring CEO should not continue on. However, in about one company in five the retired CEO does stay on. When I congratulated James Burke, retired chairman of Johnson & Johnson, on his decision not to stay on the board, he said, "It was not a difficult call to make.

All I had to do was put myself in the place of my successor—and I knew I should not stay."

As the time for retirement approaches, the outside directors, in one of their executive meetings, can agree that the retiring CEO should not stay on, and they can appoint someone to deliver the message. The successor will heave a sigh of relief—and be better motivated to develop his or her own agenda for improving company performance.*

The Time and Motivation to Serve Effectively. To be an effective and independent outside director, the person must have the time and motivation, which frequently go together. Two common sources of outside directors need careful thought: active CEOs and retired CEOs. The most common source is the active CEO from whom the chief executive and the board hope to learn, and vice versa. In addition, a director who is CEO of a prestigious company becomes a "brand name," and may even improve the stock price.

Questions: Do active CEOs have the time to serve effectively? If active CEOs serve on more than one outside board, will they have the luxury of serving under "normal" circumstances, that is, with no unusual happenings taking up extra time (such as a threatened takeover of their own company or the board company)? But doesn't something "unusual" often happen? Then aren't the outside CEOs likely to be motivated to absent themselves from board meetings, or, if they do attend, try to get the meetings over with as soon as possible?

After observing the unexpected demands on client CEOs who sit on other boards, I have to conclude that the CEO of a major or global leadership company should be careful in taking the time or giving the kind of thought that is required to serve responsibly on even one other company board.

And the time that *any* director is likely to take for board membership should be estimated. There are surveys of time requirements for board memberships, but I believe an estimate for each specific company board would not be difficult and is likely to be more accurate: the

---

*Guideline 9 provides that a former CEO serving on the board will be considered an inside director for purposes of voting on matters of corporate governance.

number and length of board meetings, number and length of committee meetings for the particular individual, travel time, and review and preparation time.

A company selecting director candidates can also estimate the time each individual already spends with *other* companies. And conversely, retired individuals who "collect" directorates should recognize that well-run companies want independent, high-performing, and really interested directors.

I also caution against having too many retired CEOs on the board. They make up a substantial percentage of the outside directors in the 1995 Fortune 100 companies. Although 15 companies had none in this category, the rest had one to seven retired CEOs, with 14 companies having four, and 55 companies having one or two.[26]

In my opinion, having multiple retired chief executives on a board does not convey a strong company image. As directors, they may have much of value to offer and, like active CEOs, their "brand names" may help the stock price. But retired CEOs may take on too many boards and not have adequate time to serve them all effectively.

In particular, "brand name" retired chief executives often sit on from seven to ten boards. And until the recent boardroom revolution, most of them apparently sat passively. How can these directors possibly have time to deliver high-caliber performance? Will their desire to continue having something to do, and being with companionable peers, make them reluctant to take strong independent action? Will they also shun independence because they want to continue their attractive flow of cash and other recent perks such as stock options and pensions?

Bob Monks, the shareholder activist, says directors should limit themselves to no more than three boards.[27] I agree.

Finding Director Candidates. The nominating committee (or committee on director affairs) does not have an easy task in finding highly competent people with independent orientations who have the time to discharge the director's duties responsibly and are also willing to accept the legal risks of being a board member. Besides providing insurance, the answer lies in broadening the hunt.

"Professional" directors are competent independent directors: individuals who devote all their time to serving on boards, seeking to develop reputations for competence and independence that qualify them to expand their clientele. Of course, the need to avoid conflicts of interest will automatically hold down the number of positions they can accept.

A client chief executive of an international company once asked me to recommend a director. But when I suggested a professional director whom I had checked and who sat on only two boards, the chief said: "I don't think he would fit. We meet in various parts of the world and bring our wives. So we have become sort of a club." That company has been taken over.

The very difficulty of the recruiting task makes it inevitable that the nominating committee (or CDA) will recommend—and the board will elect—someone who is incompetent. The danger of such a mistake flows from the custom of "once a director, always a director" (until the required retirement date is reached).

One way to deal with this problem, of course, is to establish term limits for directors. Or companies could establish processes for unseating poorly performing directors. If there is a separate board chairman, it would be his or her responsibility to tell the poor performer to shape up or ship out. I prefer term limits.

Director Shareholdings. GM has no guideline here. Since the number of shares of public company stock held by directors must be disclosed, this evidence of director interest in the company can be evaluated by employees, other directors, other shareholders, and potential shareholders.

A large shareholding by directors would, of course, indicate confidence in the future of the company, whereas shares ranging from 100 to 500 are generally seen as token holdings (not to be confused with stock options). A required shareholding would not be out of order. Bob Monks points out that "nothing makes a director think and act like a shareholder more than being a shareholder."[28]

In fact, Campbell Soup requires directors to own shares (standard

12): "Directors are required to own at least 1,000 shares within one year of election and 3,000 shares within three years of election."

Board Agenda. As defined earlier, governance is about management and the board working together to ensure effective decision making. With that as the goal, each board member should feel free to suggest agenda items. If there is a separate board chairman, members would suggest agenda topics to the chair, who would discuss them with the chief executive. Or they might be sent in advance to the lead director.

Since the board will be dealing chiefly with major long-term issues, at each board meeting the chairman could ask directors for suggestions of issues to be discussed at the next or subsequent meetings. That would give everyone time to prepare. In these ways, the agenda that would make for the best decisions for the company would be developed.

As Mr. Pearce described earlier, "Everyone can speak candidly, there's no sense of not wanting to hear something, and it doesn't matter if it's controversial."[29]

Succession Planning. Guideline 27 provides that annually the CEO will make a report to the board on succession planning, and that on a continuing basis the CEO will recommend a successor should he or she be unexpectedly disabled.

Making Major Board Decisions. There have been many serious consequences when "rubber stamp" boards have casually approved recommendations of chief executives for acquisitions, mergers, sales of subsidiaries, leveraged buyouts, and so on. If the directors carry out their responsibilities and exercise due diligence in making such important decisions, boards can earn their keep by protecting not only stockholder interests but the interests of other stakeholders as well.

For major decisions, the board needs a reasonable length of time to consider all the issues involved carefully, and to engage in constructive debate. If the chief executive says that something important is urgent, the board had better find out whether someone is pushing and has a sound basis for doing so.

For its part, management should send the board a memorandum presenting its proposal, together with an alternative (if feasible), giving the probable risks (financial, intangible, and people), and the consequences of each. The memo should give the best, worst, and most likely numbers—and conclude with management's recommendation for action.

Executive Sessions of Outside Directors. Guideline 14 provides for the outside directors to meet three times each year in executive session, with each meeting including a discussion with the CEO. This is an excellent idea.

Size of the Board. I have waited to discuss the size of the board until most of the issues affecting size were before you. Although at the time its guidelines were written the GM board had 13 members, it felt that a size of 15 would be about right. However, that board would be willing to accept a somewhat larger number to accommodate an outstanding candidate(s).

In my opinion, board membership is best kept small, thus facilitating decision making between management and the board. There need be only enough people for cross-checking: a dozen should be adequate.

The GM board's mission statement helps focus the discussion, and if the chairman is separate from the CEO, he or she will quickly become a better meeting chairman. So I believe it is wise for a leadership company to strive to keep board membership to as few as feasible.

Conclusion

Companies that wish to overhaul board structures, policies, and procedures would do well to consider the GM Guidelines, the Campbell Standards, the Harvard-based research, and the British point of view.

But, again, the conventions of board governance are less important than are the people, and the qualifications of the people, who are actually brought onto the board through the *use* of conventions. The next key factor is the effectiveness with which the board then monitors both its own performance and the performance of management. As in any aspect of running a business, guidelines and standards are important, but it is the quality of the decisions made by people as they follow the guidelines and standards that really determines company performance.

And most important of all is the policy that management and the board shall work together closely in making the major decisions that determine outstanding company performance.

Focus on the Long Term. The board should be the watchdog against "short-termism." To emphasize the board's responsibility for guarding against "short-termism," I refer to a 1992 report of the Twentieth Century Fund, developed by a task force of business leaders, academics, bankers, investment bankers, money managers, and analysts who looked at "a series of questions about our financial markets and corporate governance." The report draws this important conclusion about pressure from financial markets: "The United States economy and financial system suffer from 'short-termism,' an affliction caused by a lack of attention to long-term economic performance. Financial markets put pressure on corporate managers to focus too much on quarterly profits and too little on patient investment for the long haul."[30]

And the following passage from the report is worth careful study by executives and directors:

> The problem of short-termism is neither new nor the sort of national crisis that excites the popular imagination. After all, its effects will not be felt until some time in the future. Short-termism in finance and corporate planning, however, deserves attention because it is part of a larger pattern in which finance flourishes while our real economic foundation slowly erodes. In the 1980s, America's financial markets soared, fed by a surge of corporate takeovers and restructuring. For a while, it seemed as if financial deals alone could create real purchasing power. But even during those heady years, the real income of ordinary people stagnated. Perhaps the spotlight on financial superstars blinded the nation to such long-term, structural problems in the real economy as slow productivity growth, falling saving rates, inadequate educational and health-care systems, growing ex-

tremes of wealth and poverty, and the enormous burden of public and private debt. Today, these real economic problems threaten our standing in a world of intensifying global economic competition.[31]

Following that tour de force, however, comes this flabby statement: "The question thus is, What changes in our laws, regulatory structures, and corporate culture will help channel the skill and energy of our financial and managerial elite toward long-run performance rather than short-term appearances?"[32]

How can government require that companies make long-term decisions? The way a company is run in the United States can be determined, collectively, only by management, the board, and competition, while, of course, observing ethics and the law.

Director Compensation. Let's say the new forces and bandwagon factors operate to bring about all of the changes discussed earlier. And the board has a decision-making relationship with management, as well as a basic mission to protect the company's long-term health and to ensure its survival. The directors are carefully selected for their talent, independence, and dedication; their performance is evaluated annually.

Are these directors not entitled to compensation that is related to *their* performance? Would not all the stakeholders as well as large investors feel that such an arrangement is fair and in the interests of everyone? Would not such an arrangement help in recruiting high-talent, dedicated directors?

GM requires that its staff make an annual report to the CDA on how its board compensation compares to that of other large U.S. companies. Every company wants its board compensation to be generally competitive, but a leadership company will also want that compensation to be fair.

GM believes that a meaningful portion of a director's compensation should be provided in common stock units, and that any changes in compensation should come at the suggestion of the CDA but with full discussion with and concurrence of the board. A good idea.

Walter Salmon suggests some form of stock options. In my view, the stakeholders (including employees) in a leadership company would agree to that way of compensating directors. And representatives of each stakeholder group could participate in developing such a plan.

European Corporate Governance

Europe is in worse shape in corporate governance than the United States. For example, after an 18-year tenure as chairman, Carlo De Benedetti was required to resign from Olivetti SpA, the beleaguered Italian information technology and telecommunications company.[33] If he had been head of an American or British firm, he would have been ousted long ago. Between September 1992 and December 1993, the chairmen of seven large U.S. companies were dismissed;[34] all had tenures far shorter than De Benedetti's.

The *Financial Times*, in referring to De Benedetti's dismissal, stated, "This muscle-flexing should not only be good for Olivetti; evidence that Anglo-Saxon shareholders are taking a more active approach to underperforming continental companies could mark a defining point in European corporate governance."[35]

So European companies had better heed the U.S. forces I discussed earlier and follow the Harvard-based and General Motors recommendations for improving corporate governance. Indeed, in a competitive global world they will ultimately be forced to do so. Thus every board—U.S. and European—will ultimately have the responsibility of ensuring that the chief executive of every corporation maintains the "successful perpetuation of the business."

EPILOGUE
STARTING THE CONVERSION
PROCESS

I F YOU, the reader, are the chief executive, all you need to do to start the conversion process is talk with one of your directors. You don't have to recommend conversion—just suggest exploring it. And once you as chief executive start the process, it will take on a life of its own.

Of course, this first director can call the whole idea naive, thus killing the process at the outset. Or he or she may continue the process by saying, "Let's try getting some of our executives to experiment with learning leadership. Perhaps they will at least become better executives or managers. We can't lose by trying that."

But perhaps you, as chief executive, are reluctant to let go of authority, which gives you a feeling of security. You need not be afraid of letting go because you can easily take authority back. In fact, one of the problems of converting to leadership is that the learner of leadership slips back into exercising authority. To learn to lead, you must have the will to lead.

Three Best Bets for Conversion

What types of companies are most likely to be candidates for conversion? My research indicates that more than a few privately held companies (many of which are sizable) are often alert to new and advanced ways of running their companies—particularly in ways of treating their people better. Chief executives of these companies may be willing to try conversion because they don't have to worry about the effects on stock prices. If even a small number of these conversions are successful, they may set examples for public companies and so create a small bandwagon effect.

Leveraged buyout firms may also find that they are ready to try making leadership companies out of companies they've acquired. A principal in the buyout firm may start the conversion process simply by speaking with the chief executive of the acquired company.

And, of course, a new company could begin as a leadership company, that is, founding executives could learn leadership together instead of automatically using authority to run the business.

Other Best Bets for Conversion

Another way to stir up interest in the conversion process is to review a range of corporate situations where moving from command and control to leadership might be a risk worth taking, and then to determine whether any of these hypothetical situations matches your own company's circumstances.

Here are a few:

Company A. The CEO of this publicly held company knows he is a leader and can easily learn to become an even better leader. He is currently leading from the top but believes that a network of leaders would improve performance substantially. The CEO has eight years before retirement, adequate time to complete the conversion or, upon evaluation, to reverse it.

The CEO asks two senior executives to experiment with learning leadership on the job along with him while he is learning to improve his own leadership. After a year, these experiments are successful, and these three people at the top believe that others can learn to lead too, especially when people are learning together as part of an official program. The company has the financial resources to risk a decline in profits should there be any confusion during conversion. The board approves, and the company goes ahead.

Company B. This company is faltering, but the board believes that financial resources are adequate to take the risk of conversion. The board also concludes that conversion to a leadership company might save the business. After considering dismissal of the chairman (and CEO), the board concludes that she can learn to lead but needs the support of a chairman's team of three. The chairman and the board select two senior executives in whom they have confidence and who, they feel, can learn to lead along with the chairman.

The board meets with the members of the chairman's team; explains that they are co-leaders in a leadership team, with the chairman first among equals; and explains that the whole team has an opportunity to learn leadership together. The board tells the team that it has 18 months to show enough progress to indicate that the team can save the company. Otherwise, the board will bring in a CEO from the outside and give up the chairman's team.

With everyone recognizing that these are long-shot arrangements, the company goes ahead.

Company C. This company is faltering badly, and the board decides to bring in a new company chairman from the outside. Since the company's products are unusual, the board also decides to set up a chairman's team, so that two members of the team from the inside can help the new company chairman from the outside learn the business. The board hopes to find a company chairman who will accept the other two members as co-chairmen.

The board also elects an outside chairman of the board who agrees to spend significant time with the chairman's team to help it succeed, especially to ensure that trust and good relations exist among the three members personally.

The board recruits a new company chairman who has a good record, fine character, and attributes that should enable him to learn leadership rapidly—and who is willing that the other members of the chairman's team shall be co-chairmen. The board chairman and the chairman's team hold a number of meetings as a group and in pairs. The board chairman explains the nature of a leadership company and a chairman's team, pointing out that the company chairman is first among equals.

After these meetings, the new company chairman expresses his enthusiasm for the arrangements to the board, thereby demonstrating an important aspect of leadership ability. And the three decide they can work well together to become leaders and co-chairmen together.

With apparent trust among all involved, the new company chairman and the 2 co-chairmen are elected members of the board. The separate board chairman, 8 other independent and effective outside directors, and the chairman's team make up the board of 12.

Then, with no specific timetable, the chairman's team goes confidently forward to try out the new way of running the company, with the understanding that if it does not work out, the new company chairman will become chief executive and new arrangements will be made by the board.

This is one way to use a leadership company as a possible way of saving a faltering company.

Readers are certain to think of other ways to start the conversion process. So with these and other possibilities, I'm encouraged to believe that this book, and the reader's time in reading it, may produce useful action—even should the reader decide simply to learn additional leadership attributes and become a better executive or manager in his or her present company.

Interview of John Whitehead by Jon Katzenbach

J OHN WHITEHEAD was co-chairman, with John Weinberg, of Goldman Sachs & Company from 1976 to 1984. John Whitehead then became Deputy Secretary, Department of State, from 1985 to 1989, and is now chairman of AEA Investors. Jon Katzenbach is a director of McKinsey & Company. This interview was conducted on September 27, 1994.

K = Katzenbach; W = Whitehead

K. *John, why don't you just broadly reflect on the team activity at Goldman, as you remember it. What was significant about it, and what clients and situations do you recall?*

W. All right. We had a culture of having teams at Goldman Sachs, rather than dominant individuals. And it was because we enjoyed working in that atmosphere, in part, but also because we thought it was better business. If you have one dominant person, all the clients want to see him. And, you don't have any chance to go beyond the limits of that person's capacity.

K. *Did you typically use two-person teams, or were there larger ones?*

W. Well, at all levels of the organization, there were various sized teams. Teams that organized for particular projects, teams organized on a permanent basis, as departments or subdepartments, so that the teamwork spirit was very important. And when we recruited, we looked for people that we thought would be good team members.

And not for people with big egos that we thought would have to dominate any situation, and would want to become famous.

K. *The ego problem is one we've run into a lot, when we look at teams at the top of different sorts of organizations. Did you consciously try to screen the ego problem out of the recruiting?*

W. Yes. We looked for teamwork as being a key ingredient in the people that we offered jobs to. Would they be good team players? Would they be able to subordinate their own egos for the benefit of the firm, and the benefit of the team? We wanted our clients to think that whoever Goldman Sachs assigned to work on their project would be good. That they didn't have to get a particular person whose name might be known in order to be satisfied with our service to them.

K. *And any member of a team could satisfy that?*

W. Yes.

K. *If it worked right.*

W. Yes. Now, the origin of the co-chairman was, of course, an extension of that team culture. When John Weinberg and I took over as the joint heads of Goldman Sachs, co-equal in every way, that established an unusual arrangement for investment banking, or for any business, at that particular time. I think this was back in 1976. So it was quite a long time ago. And [before] our predecessor, Gus Levy, died, he told us that it was up to us, the two of us, to inherit the leadership of the firm. We were the next most important partners, the two of us. And we had always been co-equal, since we became partners. We sat down and decided how we should run the place. What should we do. And, instead of one of us being the boss guy and the other being a number two guy, we decided why not try to do it together, as co-equals. And both of us felt that we would be satisfied with that, and we quickly agreed to do that.

One of the most important parts of it, though, and the reason that made it so successful, was that John and I had been good friends for more than 20 years, and we'd come up in the business together. And we each saw things alike. We knew that we would be very compatible in doing it. We decided that instead of his running part of the business and my running another part of the business, as has been done by others, we would both run it together. We would both be responsible, together, for all of the business. And I think that was a very important part of the reason that it was so successful.

K. *Have you ever run into any other situation at the top that was similar to that?*

W. I don't know that anybody has really done it in exactly that same way. The tendency is to sort of divvy up the responsibilities, and one person take half of them, and the other person take the other half. But we decided that if we were to do that, we would, in effect, be in competition with each other. I would be trying to make my business predominant, and he would be trying to make his business predominant, and that really wouldn't be very good.

K. *Why do you think more organizations don't try that?*

W. Usually the fellow who thinks he's ready to be the CEO wants to do it all by himself. He believes he's ready for that, and his board of directors believes he's ready for that. And so they don't really think how much better an organization can be if two people can work together running it.

K. *But you told me that you have parallel situations down the line that are like you and John at the top?*

W. We didn't then, but they developed. In fact, the investment banking end of the business has been headed in recent years by three people. Three co-equal chairmen. And I believe that has worked extremely well. It permits you to be interchangeable; it permits one person to travel and the other to stay home; and always have a decision maker. John and I used to tell our organization that a decision of one of us was all that was necessary; that people didn't have to go to each of us. If they got a decision, they could get it from one or the other of us and if we needed to talk with each other before we made it, we would do that. That wasn't their problem. That was our problem. And it worked very well.

K. *If you were going to make a decision different from John's, you would talk to him before you made it?*

W. We probably would have talked about it before it came up, if we were any good at anticipating what problems there might be. But we knew each other so well that we knew exactly how the other was going to react. We knew what each of us considered to be extremely important, and not so important.

You know how decisions get made; sometimes you defer. If your partner feels very strongly about something, you tend to defer to him, even though you don't agree. You tend to continue the discussion and try to work out some middle-ground decision, maybe, if neither of you feels terribly strongly about the issue. But still it's one that requires a decision.

K. *Did the relationship between Steve [Friedman] and Robert [Rubin]— was it different in any significant way?*

W. I think it was very much the same. They, too, had worked closely together. After I left to go to Washington, John Weinberg continued to be the sole chairman for several years. And he really brought up Steve and Bob. They became vice chairmen together. He assigned them to work on particular problem areas of the firm, as a team, as a pair, to test out whether they could work together well. And they did, and that structure now has been in operation for some time.

K. *Can you recall team situations that didn't work out well, in contrast to the formula of those that did?*

W. I don't think we had experiences at Goldman Sachs where they didn't work well, because we were so careful about the people involved.

K. *One of the problems we encounter is that when you drop down into the lower levels of an organization, the small team seems to form more easily. By the time you get to the top, it seems to be much harder.*

W. Well, I think that's true. People's ambitions sometimes stand in the way of being willing to give up authority to someone else. To their teammate.

K. *In particular, I guess they've worked that long to get there, [that] standing back and sharing it seems like [a letdown].*

W. And probably, to some extent, competing with their teammate, all along the line, maybe because these would be the two people who had risen up to the top of the organization. And more people ought to try saying, "We want you two fellows to run it together." If there are two people where it's hard to choose, it seems to me it's a very logical succession.

K. *That's a very good thought, because you don't lose too much if you try. So what do you do then? Then you pick a leader. But you didn't lose anything by trying.*

W. Right. Have I ever told you the story about Marvin Bower's reaction? When it was announced in the newspapers that John and I were going to be co-chairmen, Marvin Bower called up and asked if he could come and see us. We had both known Marvin, and really revered him. He was a decade or more older than we were, and he was a very important figure in our lives for both of us. So we were delighted to invite him to lunch.

And he came to lunch and he said he wanted to congratulate us both, that he'd known each of us, separately and together, for many years, and how much he admired Goldman Sachs. And he just wanted to wish us well. But he said, the trouble is, it'll never work. It goes against all the principles of management that I've learned through my whole, long career in management consulting. And he said, it's just not going to work.

K. *You will love the tag line. Do you know what Marvin is doing as we speak?*

W. No.

K. *He is in the middle of a book, which is focused on a notion of leadership teams, and he has come completely around.*

W. Has he really? Well, that's interesting.

K. *He is now writing a book about why leadership teams are more effective.*

W. That's very interesting.

K. *Today you see more and more people thinking about it.*

W. I think that's true. We never had an occasion where we had a real disagreement between us. I think maybe the only times that there were differences were in our appraisal of people. Every once in a while, I would have a higher opinion of somebody than he would, or he had a higher opinion of somebody than I would. And then we had to talk that out. But I believe that where we had those differences, we arrived at better conclusions, because we did talk about that and we had two points of view, two minds, setting on the problem. And knowing [we] had to end up making a decision, and not just a recommendation to someone else.

K. *Roughly how much time would the two of you spend together?*

W. Not as much as you might think. We both traveled a lot. And we tried—although we didn't always succeed—to have one of us in the office, and the other of us traveling. We gave that up after a while. But we talked, certainly, once a day and tried to keep each other posted on what was going on. And, of course, we got a flow of information from inside the firm that helped us manage what we both saw and both absorbed. And that provided a sort of basis for our decision making, as well as our talking with each other.

K. *Did you work together in client situations?*

W. Very rarely. That was one of the big advantages We didn't allow a client to get to know us both. They could have one or the other, but they couldn't have both. And that was the advantage of co-chairmanship. I don't remember anybody ever insisting that they wanted to talk to both of us together. One was enough. And, maybe it's more than enough. (Laughter)

K. *Any other advice you would give top managements today, as they contemplate whether they could work more in the team mode as opposed to the individual mode? What would you advise?*

W. Well, I think I would certainly urge people to adopt the team concept. It is alien to many people's concept of what business organizations are about.

I think the average person thinks that business is extremely competitive, and sort of cutthroat, and people are out to upstage each other all the time. And people don't really want to work under those circumstances. And if you are going to be happy in your job, every day, you certainly have a happier situation if you're part of a team, and the team is working, and you're cooperating with each other. Instead of looking to your own self-aggrandizement.

K. *There's a real job satisfaction advantage.*

W. Much, much, much greater. And I think that starts with teams at the lower level, that work on individual projects, right up to the top. I certainly enjoyed it. I got every bit of satisfaction that one could possibly get out of being the co-chairman. I never once really wished that I could do it all myself or get all the credit, because there were so many benefits that came from there being two of us.

K. *And I guess one of the benefits is that when trouble strikes, you have someone there with you.*

W. Absolutely right, absolutely.

K. *And most CEOs are all alone.*

W. Absolutely. And we complemented each other. I was better at some things than John was, and John was better than I was at other things. And when we had a particular kind of problem, I quickly said, You handle this one. (Laughs) This one is in your bailiwick. And there were other times when he would defer to me. It was a constant matter of using each other's strengths and weaknesses. And when you have two sets of strengths at the top, you're more likely to be right than wrong, I think.

K. *Any predictions about where Goldman will go with the next wave of leadership?*

W. Well, I broke up John's and my team by going to Washington, although, in my case, I really retired before I knew I was going to Washington. I decided that the time had come. I was three years older than John, and we didn't want to both go together. That would have been bad. So, it was up to me to go first, and I picked what I thought was a good time.

John, then, was the sole chairman for several years and then Steve and Bob became co-chairmen. That worked just as well as John's and mine worked. Then Bob Rubin went off to Washington. Poor Steve was left all by himself. But now, Steve is retiring at the end of this year and he has appointed another pair—a third pair—of co-chairmen. And, I believe John Corzine and Hank Paulsen will be co-chairmen for the next generation. I hope for a good long time.

K. *Have they had the same opportunity to work together that I know you and John had?*

W. In preparing, John Weinberg took a lot of chances or opportunities to get Steve and Bob to work together.

K. *Will the next two have had that same [opportunity]?*

W. They have had the same opportunity to work together to see how they complemented each other, and they passed those tests very well. So, I'm very optimistic as to how it will work.

K. *Thank you, John, for sharing your perspective on what has been a fantastic part of your business history in a great institution.*

W. Well, thanks. You're welcome.

GM Board of Directors
Corporate Governance Guidelines

(INDEX)

14. Executive sessions of outside Directors

15. Assessing the Board's performance

16. Board's interaction with institutional investors, press, customers, etc.

Board Relationship to Senior Management

17. Regular attendance of non-Directors at Board meetings

18. Board access to senior management

Meeting Procedures

19. Selection of agenda items for Board meetings

20. Board materials distributed in advance

21. Board presentations

Committee Matters

22. Number, structure, and independence of Committees

23. Assignment and rotation of Committee members

24. Frequency and length of Committee meetings

25. Committee agenda

Leadership Development

26. Formal evaluation of the Chief Executive Officer

27. Succession planning

28. Management development

THE MISSION OF THE GENERAL MOTORS BOARD OF DIRECTORS

The General Motors Board of Directors represents the owners' interest in perpetuating a successful business, including optimizing long term financial returns. The Board is responsible for determining that the Corporation is managed in such a way to ensure this result. This is an active, not a passive, responsibility. The Board has the responsibility to ensure that in good times, as well as difficult ones, Management is capably executing its responsibilities. The Board's responsibility is to regularly monitor the effectiveness of Management policies and decisions including the execution of its strategies.

In addition to fulfilling its obligations for increased stockholder value, the Board has responsibility to GM's customers, employees, suppliers and to the communities where it operates—all of whom are essential to a successful business. All of these responsibilities, however, are founded upon the successful perpetuation of the business.

GUIDELINES ON SIGNIFICANT CORPORATE GOVERNANCE ISSUES

Selection and Composition of the Board

1. **Board Membership Criteria.** The Committee on Director Affairs is responsible for reviewing with the Board, on an annual basis, the appropriate skills and characteristics required of Board members in the context of the current make-up of the Board. This assessment should include issues of diversity, age, skills such as understanding of manufacturing technologies, international background, etc.—all in the context of an assessment of the perceived needs of the Board at that point in time.

2. **Selection and Orientation of New Directors.** The Board itself should be responsible, in fact as well as procedure, for selecting its own members and in recommending them for election by the stockholders. The Board delegates the screening process involved to the Committee on Director Affairs with the direct input from the Chairman of the Board, as well as the Chief Executive Officer. The Board and the Company have a complete orientation process for new Directors that includes background material, meetings with senior management and visits to Company facilities.

3. **Extending the Invitation to a Potential Director to Join the Board.** The invitation to join the Board should be extended by the Board itself, by the Chairman of the Committee on Director Affairs (if the Chairman and CEO hold the same position), the Chairman of the Board, and the Chief Executive Officer of the Company.

Board Leadership

4. Selection of Chairman and CEO. The Board should be free to make this choice any way that seems best for the Company at a given point in time.

Therefore, the Board does not have a policy, one way or the other, on whether or not the role of the Chief Executive and Chairman should be separate and, if it is to be separate, whether the Chairman should be selected from the non-employee Directors or be an employee.

5. Lead Director Concept. The Board adopted a policy that it have a Director selected by the outside Directors who will assume the responsibility of chairing the regularly scheduled meetings of outside Directors or other responsibilities which the outside Directors as a whole might designate from time to time.

Currently, this role is filled by the non-executive Chairman of the Board. Should the Company be organized in such a way that the Chairman is an employee of the Company, another Director would be selected for this responsibility.

Board Composition and Performance

6. Size of the Board. The Board presently has thirteen members. It is the sense of the Board that a size of fifteen is about right. However, the Board would be willing to go to a somewhat larger size in order to accommodate the availability of an outstanding candidate(s).

7. Mix of Inside and Outside Directors. The Board believes that as a matter of policy, there should be a majority of independent Directors on the GM Board (as stipulated in By-law 2.12). The Board is willing to have members of Management, in addition to the Chief Executive Officer, as Directors. But, the Board believes that Management should encourage senior managers to understand that Board membership is not necessary or a prerequisite to any higher management position in the Company. Managers other than the Chief Executive Officer currently attend Board meetings on a regular basis even though they are not members of the Board.

On matters of corporate governance, the Board assumes decisions will be made by the outside Directors.

8. Board Definition of What Constitutes Independence for Outside Directors. GM's By-law defining independent Directors was approved by the Board in January 1991. The Board believes there is no current relationship between any outside Director and GM that would be construed in any way to compromise any Board member being designated independent. Compliance with the By-law is reviewed annually by the Committee on Director Affairs.

9. Former Chief Executive Officer's Board Membership. The Board believes this is a matter to be decided in each individual instance. It is assumed that when the Chief Executive Officer resigns from that position, he/she should submit his/her resignation from the Board at the same time. Whether the individual continues to serve on the Board is a matter for discussion at that time with the new Chief Executive Officer and the Board.

A former Chief Executive Officer serving on the Board will be considered an inside Director for purposes of voting on matters of corporate governance.

10. Directors Who Change Their Present Job Responsibility. It is the sense of the Board that individual Directors who change the responsibility they held when they were elected to the Board should submit a letter of resignation to the Board. It is not the sense of the Board that in every instance the Directors who retire or change from the position they held when they came on the Board should necessarily leave the Board. There should, however, be an opportunity for the Board, via the Committee on Director Affairs, to review the continued appropriateness of Board membership under these circumstances.

11. Term Limits. The Board does not believe it should establish term limits. While term limits could help insure that there are fresh ideas and viewpoints available to the Board, they hold the disadvantage of losing the contribution of Directors who have been able to develop, over a period of time, increasing insight into the company and its operations and, therefore, provide an increasing contribution to the Board as a whole.

As an alternative to term limits, the Committee on Director Affairs, in conjunction with the Chief Executive Officer and the Chairman of the Board, will formally review each Director's continuation on the Board every five years. This will also allow each Director the opportunity to conveniently confirm his/her desire to continue as a member of the Board.

12. Retirement Age. It is the sense of the Board that the current retirement age of 70 is appropriate.

13. Board Compensation Review. It is appropriate for the staff of the Company to report once a year to the Committee on Director Affairs the status of GM Board compensation in relation to other large U.S. companies. As part of a Director's total compensation and to create a direct linkage with corporate performance, the Board believes that a meaningful portion of a Director's compensation should be provided in common stock units.

Changes in Board compensation, if any, should come at the suggestion of the Committee on Director Affairs, but with full discussion and concurrence by the Board.

14. Executive Sessions of Outside Directors. The outside Directors of the Board will meet in Executive Session three times each year. The format of these meetings will include a discussion with the Chief Executive Officer on each occasion.

15. Assessing the Board's Performance. The Committee on Director Affairs is responsible to report annually to the Board an assessment of the Board's performance. This will be discussed with the full Board. This should be done following the end of each fiscal year and at the same time as the report on Board membership criteria.

This assessment should be of the Board's contribution as a whole and specifically review areas in which the Board and/or the Management believes a better contribution could be made. Its purpose is to increase the effectiveness of the Board, not to target individual Board members.

16. Board's Interaction with Institutional Investors, Press, Customers, Etc. The Board believes that the Management speaks for General Motors. Individual Board members may, from time to time at the request of the Management, meet or otherwise communicate with various constituencies that are involved with General Motors. If comments from the Board are appropriate, they should, in most circumstances, come from the Chairman.

Board Relationship to Senior Management

17. Regular Attendance of Non-Directors at Board Meetings. The Board welcomes the regular attendance at each Board meeting of non-Board members who are members of the President's Council.

Should the Chief Executive Officer want to add additional people as attendees on a regular basis, it is expected that this suggestion would be made to the Board for its concurrence.

18. Board Access to Senior Management. Board members have complete access to GM's Management. It is assumed that Board members will use judgment to be sure that this contact is not distracting to the business operation of the Company and that such contact, if in writing, be copied to the Chief Executive and the Chairman.

Furthermore, the Board encourages the management to, from time to time, bring managers into Board meetings who: (a) can provide additional insight into the items being discussed because of personal involvement in these areas, and/or (b) represent managers with future potential that the senior management believes should be given exposure to the Board.

Meeting Procedures

19. Selection of Agenda Items for Board Meetings. The Chairman of the Board and the Chief Executive Officer (if the Chairman is not the Chief Executive Officer) will establish the agenda for each Board meeting.

Each Board member is free to suggest the inclusion of item(s) on the agenda.

20. Board Materials Distributed in Advance. It is the sense of the Board that information and data that is important to the Board's understanding of the business be distributed in writing to the Board before the Board meets. The Management will make every attempt to see that this material is as brief as possible while still providing the desired information.

21. Board Presentations. As a general rule, presentations on specific subjects should be sent to the Board members in advance so that Board meeting time may be conserved and discussion time focused on questions that the Board has about the material. On those occasions in which the subject matter is too sensitive to put on paper, the presentation will be discussed at the meeting.

Committee Matters

22. Number, Structure and Independence of Committees. The current Committee structure of the Company seems appropriate. There will, from time to time, be occasions in which the Board may want to form a new Committee or disband a current Committee depending upon the circumstances. The current six Committees are Audit, Capital Stock, Director Affairs, Finance, Executive Compensation and Public Policy. The Committee membership, with the exception of the Finance Committee, will consist only of independent Directors as stipulated in By-law 2.12.

23. Assignment and Rotation of Committee Members. The Committee on Director Affairs is responsible, after consultation with the Chief Executive Officer and with consideration of the desires of individual Board members, for the assignment of Board members to various Committees.

It is the sense of the Board that consideration should be given to rotating Committee members periodically at about a five-year interval, but the Board does not feel that such a rotation should be mandated as a policy since there may be reasons at a given point in time to maintain an individual Director's Committee membership for a longer period.

24. Frequency and Length of Committee Meetings. The Committee Chairman, in consultation with Committee members, will determine the frequency and length of the meetings of the Committee.

25. Committee Agenda. The Chairman of the Committee, in consultation with the appropriate members of Management and staff, will develop the Committee's agenda.

Each Committee will issue a schedule of agenda subjects to be discussed for the ensuing year at the beginning of each year (to the degree these can be foreseen). This forward agenda will also be shared with the Board.

Leadership Development

26. Formal Evaluation of the Chief Executive Officer. The full Board (outside Directors) should make this evaluation annually, and it should be communicated to the Chief Executive Officer by the (non-executive) Chairman of the Board or the Lead Director.

The evaluation should be based on objective criteria including performance of the business, accomplishment of long-term strategic objectives, development of Management, etc.

The evaluation will be used by the Executive Compensation Committee in the course of its deliberations when considering the compensation of the Chief Executive Officer.

27. Succession Planning. There should be an annual report by the Chief Executive Officer to the Board on succession planning.

There should also be available, on a continuing basis, the Chief Executive Officer's recommendation as a successor should he/she be unexpectedly disabled.

28. Management Development. There should be an annual report to the Board by the Chief Executive Officer on the Company's program for Management development.

This report should be given to the Board at the same time as the succession planning report noted previously.

NOTES

PROLOGUE

1. John Pound, "The Promise of the Governed Corporation," *Harvard Business Review*, March–April 1995, 92.
2. Marvin Bower, *The Will to Manage: Corporate Success Through Programmed Management* (New York: McGraw-Hill, 1966), 250–252.
3. Stratford Sherman, "How Tomorrow's Best Leaders Are Learning Their Stuff," *Fortune*, November 27, 1995, 90.

CHAPTER ONE

1. Alfred D. Chandler, Jr., *Strategy and Structure: Chapters in the History of the American Industrial Enterprise* (Boston: M.I.T. Press, 1962).
2. General Electric 1991 Letter to Share Owners, February 14, 1992, 2.
3. Elmer W. Johnson, "An Insider's Call for Outside Direction," *Harvard Business Review*, March–April 1990, 46.
4. PepsiCo 1991 Letter from the Chairman, 1992, 4.
5. Allied-Signal 1991 Letter to Shareowners, February 10, 1992, 1.
6. Alcoa 1991 Letter to Shareholders, February 14, 1992, 2.

CHAPTER TWO

1. In 1995, A. T. Kearney sold out to Electronic Data Systems Corp., then a unit of General Motors but later separated from GM.

CHAPTER THREE

1. Ron Daniel, remarks to a conference of McKinsey partners, Washington, D.C., April 1985.
2. Pearl S. Buck, lecture for the Ghandi Foundation, Washington, D.C., April 23, 1960.
3. James Q. Wilson, *The Moral Sense* (New York: The Free Press, 1993).
4. From biographical information provided to the producer of the "Horatio Alger Awards" television show, 1994.
5. Wilson, *The Moral Sense*, 60.
6. Robert K. Greenleaf, *Servant Leadership* (New York: Paulist Press, 1977).
7. Walter Kiechel III, "The Leader as Servant," *Fortune*, May 4, 1992, 121.

8. "I.B.M. May Quit Hilltop Headquarters," *New York Times,* January 13, 1994.

9. *60 Minutes,* vol. 23, no. 20, January 27, 1991.

10. Thomas J. Peters and Robert H. Waterman, Jr., *In Search of Excellence: Lessons from America's Best-Run Companies* (New York: Harper & Row, 1982).

11. Ralph G. Nichols and Leonard A. Stevens, "Listening to People," *Harvard Business Review,* September–October 1957, 85.

12. Peter Nulty, "The National Business Hall of Fame," *Fortune,* April 4, 1994, 118.

13. Wendell L. Willkie, *One World* (New York: Simon and Schuster, 1943), 204.

14. John W. Gardner, *On Leadership* (New York: The Free Press, 1990), 49.

15. "Macy's Asks Court to Provide Shield Against Creditors," *New York Times,* January 28, 1992.

16. "Some Manufacturers Drop Efforts to Adopt Japanese Techniques," *Wall Street Journal,* May 7, 1993.

17. "Westinghouse to Lay Off 3,400, Cut Dividend," *New York Times,* January 12, 1994.

18. John W. Gardner, "Attributes and Context," *Leadership Papers/6* (published for Independent Sector, 1987), 15.

CHAPTER FOUR

1. John W. Gardner, "The Tasks of Leadership," *Leadership Papers/2,* 11.

2. John W. Gardner, *On Leadership* (New York: The Free Press, 1990), 127.

CHAPTER FIVE

1. James O. McKinsey, *Budgetary Control* (New York: The Ronald Press, 1922).

2. Ibid., 418.

3. Robert H. Waterman, Jr., *What America Does Right: Learning from Companies That Put People First* (New York: W. W. Norton & Company, 1994), 38.

4. Sam Walton, *Made in America: My Story* (New York: Doubleday, 1992), 126.

5. Alfred L. Kroeber, *Anthropology: Race-Language-Culture-Psychology-Prehistory* (New York: Harcourt, Brace and Company, 1948), 288–290.

6. "Costly Lesson: GE Finds Running Kidder, Peabody & Co. Isn't All That Easy," *Wall Street Journal,* January 27, 1989.

7. Ibid.

8. Thomas J. Watson, Jr., *A Business and Its Beliefs: The Ideas That Helped Build IBM* (New York: McGraw-Hill, 1963), McKinsey Foundation Lectures, sponsored by the Graduate School of Business, Columbia University, 5.

9. "Gerstner Is Struggling as He Tries to Change Ingrained IBM Culture," *Wall Street Journal,* May 13, 1994.

10. Joseph L. Badaracco, Jr., and Richard R. Ellsworth, *Leadership and the Quest for Integrity* (Boston, Mass.: Harvard Business School Press, 1989), 81.

11. Thomas R. Horton, *What Works for Me: 16 CEOs Talk About Their Careers and Commitments* (New York: Random House Business Division, 1986), 20.

12. Sir Adrian Cadbury, "Ethical Managers Make Their Own Rules," *Harvard Business Review*, September–October 1987, 69–73. The article was the 1986 winner of the Ethics in Business Prize for the best original article by a corporate manager on the ethical problems business executives face.

13. Harvey Golub, "Ethics: Sure It's Easy to Say That You're Pure, but Just Try Teaching Your Employees Right from Wrong," *Business Month*, October 1990, 72. Excerpted with permission, *Business Month*, October, 1990. Copyright 1990 by Goldhirsh Group, Inc., 38 Commercial Wharf, Boston, MA 02110.

14. Joyce C. Hall, *When You Care Enough* (Kansas City, Mo.: Hallmark Cards, 1979, 1992), 196.

15. Konosuke Matsushita, *Not for Bread Alone: A Business Ethos, A Management Ethic* (Kyoto, Japan: PHP Institute, 1984), 14.

16. Walton, *Made in America*, 10.

17. American Express 1995 Letter to Shareholders, February 26, 1996, 4.

18. Johnson & Johnson 1987 Letter to Stockholders, March 18, 1988, 1.

CHAPTER SIX

1. Jon R. Katzenbach and Douglas K. Smith, "Why Teams Matter," *McKinsey Quarterly*, no. 3 (1992), 3–4, based on *The Wisdom of Teams*.

2. "Pressure Growing at Disney," *New York Times*, July 18, 1994.

3. "Hollywood's Top Talent Agent Is Named as President of Disney," *New York Times*, August 15, 1995.

4. "Disney Chief Says Hiring of Ovitz Was a Mistake," *New York Times*, February 26, 1997.

CHAPTER SEVEN

1. Irvine O. Hockaday, Jr., "The Lamplighter CEO," *Chief Executive*, March 1993, 31.

2. "Compaq Storms the PC Heights from Its Factory Floor," *New York Times*, November 13, 1994.

3. Myron Magnet, "The New Golden Rule of Business," *Fortune*, February 21, 1994, 61.

4. Ibid., 60.

5. Richard N. Foster, *Innovation: The Attacker's Advantage* (New York: Summit Books, 1986), 115.

6. "A Tough Bank Boss Takes On Computers, with Real Trepidation," *Wall Street Journal*, July 25, 1996.

7. Foster, *Innovation*, 115.

8. Thomas A. Stewart, "Managing in a Wired Company," *Fortune*, July 11, 1994, 46.

9. Ibid.

10. Rick Tetzeli, "Surviving Information Overload," *Fortune*, July 11, 1994, 60.

11. Alan Deutschman with Rick Tetzeli, "Your Desktop in the Year 1996," *Fortune*, July 11, 1994, 86.

12. Amar Bhide, "Hustle as Strategy," *Harvard Business Review*, September–October 1986, 59–65.

13. Ronald Henkoff, "Delivering the Goods," *Fortune*, November 28, 1994, 64.

14. Ibid.

15. Alfred C. DeCrane, Jr., "How to Be Clean *and* Cost-Effective," *Chief Executive*, September 1992, 56.

16. Christopher A. Bartlett and Sumantra Ghoshal, "Changing the Role of Top Management: Beyond Strategy to Purpose," *Harvard Business Review*, November–December 1994, 79–88.

CHAPTER EIGHT

1. Peter Nulty, "America's Toughest Bosses," *Fortune*, February 27, 1989, 40.

2. New York Times Special Report, *The Downsizing of America* (New York: Times Books/Random House, 1996), 5.

3. "I.B.M.'s Chief Criticizes Staff Again," *New York Times*, June 19, 1991.

4. IBM 1992 Annual Meeting Report, June 10, 1992, 3.

5. Robert Levering and Milton Moskowitz, *The 100 Best Companies to Work for in America* (New York: Currency, Doubleday, 1993), dust jacket.

6. New York Times Special Report, *The Downsizing of America*, 5.

7. Ibid., 8.

8. Ibid., xiii.

9. Ibid., 18–21.

10. "Procter & Gamble in 12% Job Cut as Brand Names Lose Attraction," *New York Times*, July 16, 1993.

11. Levering and Moskowitz, *The 100 Best Companies*, 182–186.

12. Ibid., 94–97.

13. John Deere & Company 1994 Annual Report, Letter to the Stockholders, December 7, 1994, 4.

14. Levering and Moskowitz, *The 100 Best Companies*, 209.

15. Johnson & Johnson 1995 Annual Report, Letter to Stockholders, March 12, 1996, 1.

16. Peter Nulty, "The National Business Hall of Fame," *Fortune*, April 5, 1993, 112.

17. Levering and Moskowitz, *The 100 Best Companies*, 102–107.

18. "The Right Family Values in the Workplace," *Business Week*, June 28, 1993, 134.

19. "Work & Family," *Business Week,* June 28, 1993, 81–82.

20. Ibid., 82.

21. Ronald Henkoff, "Companies That Train Best," *Fortune,* March 22, 1993, 62.

22. Ibid., 62.

23. Ibid., 75.

24. Sam Walton, *Made in America: My Story* (New York: Doubleday, 1992), 127–128.

25. Ibid., 129–132.

26. Ibid., 135.

27. "Special Report on Executive Pay," *Wall Street Journal,* April 22, 1992.

28. Graef S. Crystal, *In Search of Excess: The Overcompensation of American Executives* (New York: W. W. Norton & Company, 1991), 241.

29. Ibid., 27.

30. Ibid., 28.

31. Ibid., 24.

32. Arch Patton, "The Making of Multimillion-Dollar Executives," *Business Horizons,* May–June 1994, 37.

33. Levering and Moskowitz, *The 100 Best Companies,* 291–295.

34. Janice Castro, "Disposable Workers," *Time,* March 29, 1993, 46.

CHAPTER NINE

1. "Battling for Hearts and Minds at Time Warner," *New York Times,* February 26, 1995.

2. "Morrison Knudsen Files for Protection from Its Creditors," *Wall Street Journal,* June 26, 1996.

3. "Agee Payout May Exceed $2.46 Million," *Wall Street Journal,* February 15, 1995.

4. Ibid.

5. John Pound, "The Promise of the Governed Corporation," *Harvard Business Review,* March–April 1995, 89–98.

6. Ibid., 90.

7. Ibid., 91.

8. Judith H. Dobrzynski, "Tales from the Boardroom Wars," *Business Week,* June 6, 1994, 71.

9. Robert A. G. Monks and Nell Minow, *Watching the Watchers: Corporate Governance for the 21st Century* (Cambridge, Mass.: Blackwell Publishers, 1996), 190–198.

10. "Big Investor Talked, Grace Listened," *New York Times,* April 10, 1995.

11. Ibid.

12. Judith H. Dobrzynski, "At GM, a Magna Carta for Directors," *Business Week,* April 4, 1994, 37.

13. Ibid.

14. Dissenting opinion of Chief Justice William Rehnquist in *First National Bank of Boston v. Bellotti* 435 U.S. 265, 825, 826, Sup. Ct. 1978.

15. Monks and Minow, *Watching the Watchers,* 191.

16. Pound, "The Promise," 93.

17. McKinsey research.

18. "Chairman to Step Down in G.M. Shift," *New York Times,* December 5, 1995.

19. "GM Cuts Bonuses of Top Executives, Citing Unmet Goals Despite '95 Profit," *Wall Street Journal,* April 10, 1996.

20. Walter J. Salmon, "Crisis Prevention: How to Gear Up Your Board," *Harvard Business Review,* January–February 1993, 68–75.

21. Hugh Parker, "The Chairman/CEO Separation: View One," *Directors & Boards* 18, no. 3 (Spring 1994): 45.

22. Hugh Parker, "Re-Empowering The Board," *Directors & Boards* 20, no. 2 (Winter 1996): 5.

23. Parker, "The Chairman/CEO Separation," 45.

24. "As He Steps Down, G.M. Chairman Looks Ahead," *New York Times,* December 8, 1995.

25. "Chairman to Step Down in G.M. Shift," *New York Times,* December 5, 1995.

26. McKinsey research.

27. Monks and Minow, *Watching the Watchers,* 301.

28. Parker, "Re-Empowering the Board," 10.

29. Dobrzynski, "At GM," *Business Week,* April 4, 1994, 37.

30. *The Report of The Twentieth Century Fund Task Force on Market Speculation and Corporate Governance* (New York: The Twentieth Century Fund Press, 1992), 3.

31. Ibid., 3–4.

32. Ibid., 4.

33. "Olivetti Chairman De Benedetti Quits; CEO to Lead Firm out of PC Business," *Wall Street Journal,* September 4, 1996.

34. Monks and Minow, *Watching the Watchers,* 191.

35. "Olivetti's Wake-up Call," *Financial Times,* August 30, 1996.

WORTHWHILE READING

Following are nine books from which I've drawn in making my case for the leadership company. I believe they will be useful reading for those who wish to consider converting a business from commanding to leading.

On Leadership by John W. Gardner (New York: The Free Press, 1990) (199 pages)

> A comprehensive and readable reference work on leadership by a distinguished scholar who has held many important leadership positions. He is now professor at Stanford Business School.

The Wisdom of Teams: Creating the High-Performance Organization by Jon R. Katzenbach and Douglas K. Smith (Boston: Harvard Business School Press, 1993) (265 pages)

> Provides a comprehensive reference work on teams, which are important to running a business with a network of leaders. Includes an Appendix of teams researched for the book and Selected Readings.

Made in America: My Story by Sam Walton with John Huey (New York: Doubleday, 1992) (262 pages)

> John Kotter and Jim Heskett rate Wal-Mart highly for its strong culture. Sam tells how he built the world's largest retail business in his own lifetime. And without intending to do so, he shows how he learned to be a leader. Charming reading.

"What Works for Me": 16 CEOs Talk About Their Careers and Commitments by Thomas R. Horton (New York: Random House Business Division, 1986) (400 pages)

> From 16 interviews Tom Horton has distilled 18 management

competencies and five qualities of successful CEOs. Includes count-less references to managing and many on leading. Here are the CEOs he interviewed:

James E. Burke, Johnson & Johnson
Marisa Bellisario, Italtel Societa Telecommunicazioni
J. Willard Marriott, Jr., Marriott Corporation
James M. Guinan, Caldor
James R. Martin, Massachusetts Mutual Life Insurance Company
Peter G. Scotese, Springs Industries, Inc.
Theodore M. Hesburgh C.S.C., University of Notre Dame
Harold Burson, Burson-Marsteller
Frank T. Cary, International Business Machines Corporation
Charlotte L. Beers, Tatham-Laird & Kudner
Richard A. Zimmerman, Hershey Foods Corporation
William J. Kennedy III, North Carolina Mutual Life Insurance
     Company
Henry B. Schacht, Cummins Engine Company, Inc.
Portia Isaacson, Intellisys Corporation
Ichiro Hattori, Seiko Instruments & Electronics Ltd.
Anthony J. F. O'Reilly, H. J. Heinz Company

Leadership and the Quest for Integrity by Joseph L. Badaracco, Jr., and
     Richard R. Ellsworth (Boston: Harvard Business School Press,
     1989) (209 pages)

Drawing from their extensive interviewing of CEOs, the authors present many insightful observations on leadership and integrity. See passages on pages 34, 81, 102–103, 173, and 209.

Corporate Cultures: The Rites and Rituals of Corporate Life by Terrance
     E. Deal and Allen A. Kennedy (Reading, Mass.: Addison-Wesley,
     1982) (paperback, 196 pages)

The goal of this book is "to provide business leaders with a primer on cultural management." See especially "The Importance of Understanding Culture" (pages 15–19). A good starter on an important subject.

Corporate Culture and Performance by John P. Kotter and James L. Heskett (New York: The Free Press, 1992) (151 pages)

This short book deals extensively with the cultures of leading companies and can be helpful to managers as well as to leaders. It provides excellent guidelines for a flexible network of leaders. Good bibliography.

The 100 Best Companies to Work for in America by Robert Levering and Milton Moskowitz (New York: Currency Doubleday, 1993) (498 pages)

This book, which is described in the text, would be a good reference for those designing a leadership company.

Business As a Calling: Work and the Examined Life by Michael Novak (New York: The Free Press, 1996) (237 pages)

"Michael Novak is our finest—and wisest—writer on the intricate interplay between religion and economics in American life." William E. Simon, former Secretary of the Treasury.

"This is easily the best book ever written on business as a vocation from a religious point of view. It is both thoughtful, and practical, a rare combination." Irving Kristol.

Good bibliography.

Index

ABOUT THE AUTHOR

MARVIN BOWER is a director and former managing director of McKinsey & Company, a professional management consulting firm with 69 offices around the world.

After graduating from Brown University, he earned a JD from Harvard Law School and an MBA from Harvard Business School, and joined the firm now known as Jones, Day, Reavis and Pogue, the leading corporate law firm in Cleveland, Ohio (where he grew up).

His extracurricular activities include being a trustee of Brown University, a member of the Associates of Harvard Business School, and a trustee of Case Institute of Technology. After the merger that formed Case Western Reserve University, he continued as a trustee and for a short time served as chairman of the board.

Mr. Bower was also chairman of the National Council on Economic Education, trustee of the Committee for Economic Development, director of Religion in American Life, and founding president of the Institute of Management Consultants.

He was elected to the U.S. National Business Hall of Fame, awarded the Harvard Medal, and named Fellow of the International Academy of Management. The Marvin Bower Professor of Leadership Development at Harvard Business School was established by the school in 1995, with funding from McKinsey.

Mr. Bower is the author of *The Will to Manage* and editor of *Development of Executive Leadership.*